The RAILROADER'S Wife

Letters from the Grand Trunk Pacific Railway

The RAILROADER'S Wife

Letters from the Grand Trunk Pacific Railway

JANE STEVENSON

CAITLIN PRESS

Caitlin Press Inc.
8100 Alderwood Road,
Halfmoon Bay, BC V0N 1Y1
www.caitlin-press.com

Edited by Vici Johnstone and Erin Schopfer.
Text and cover design by Michelle Winegar.
Map and train illustrations by Hans Saefkow.
Cover image Bulkley Valley Museum, P0500.
Benice Medbury Martin's letters and photos were published with the kind permission of the Bulkley Valley
Museum and Archives.

Printed in Canada on recycled paper.

Caitlin Press Inc. acknowledges the financial support of the Government of Canada through the Canada
Book Fund, the Canada Council for the Arts, and the Province of British Columbia through the British
Columbia Arts Council and the Book Publisher's Tax Credit.

Canada Council   Conseil des Arts
for the Arts   du Canada

BRITISH COLUMBIA
ARTS COUNCIL
We acknowledge the support of the Province of British Columbia
through the British Columbia Arts Council

Library and Archives Canada Cataloguing in Publication

Stevenson, Jane, 1977-
          The railroader's wife: letters from the Grand
Trunk #8232, Pacific Railway / Jane Stevenson.

ISBN 978-1-894759-43-4

          1. Martin, Bernice Medbury—Correspondence.
2. Railroads—British Columbia, Northern—Design and
construction—History. 3. Railroads—British Columbia,
Northern—History. 4. Grand Trunk Pacific Railway
Company—History. 5. British Columbia, Northern—Biography.
I. Title.

HE2809.B7S74 2010   385.09711'8   C2010-900678-X

Sincere gratitude to Mrs. Lesley Ann Vaniman,
the daughter of Bernice and Leslie Martin,
for transcribing and donating her mother's letters
to the Bulkley Valley Museum.

And to Bernice Medbury Martin.
Thank you for the adventurous spirit that brought you to northern BC
at a time of rock blasting and rail grading.

Contents

8   MAP

11   NOTE FROM THE AUTHOR

13   BEGINNINGS

19   WINTER 1912

44   SPRING 1912

60   SUMMER 1912

76   FALL 1912

95   WINTER 1912–13

112   SPRING 1913

129   SUMMER 1913

149   FALL 1913

160   WINTER 1913–14

172   SPRING 1914

183   ENDINGS

190   GLOSSARY

194   REFERENCES

198   INDEX

200   ACKNOWLEDGEMENTS

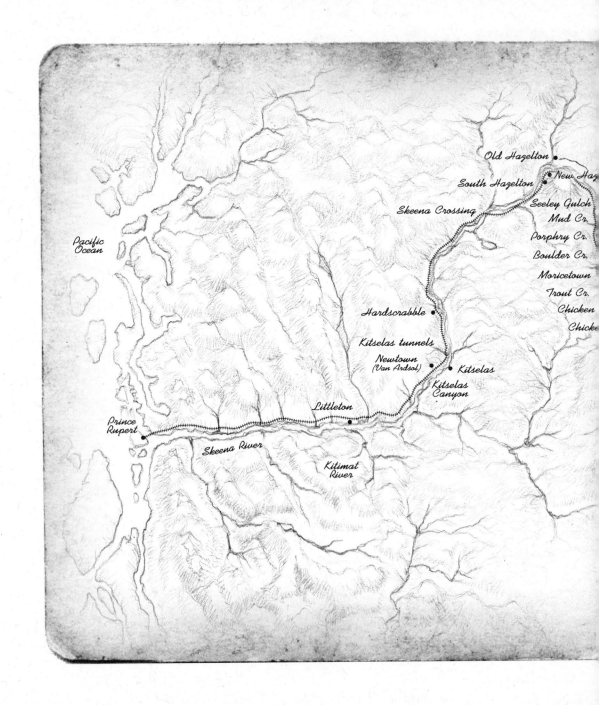

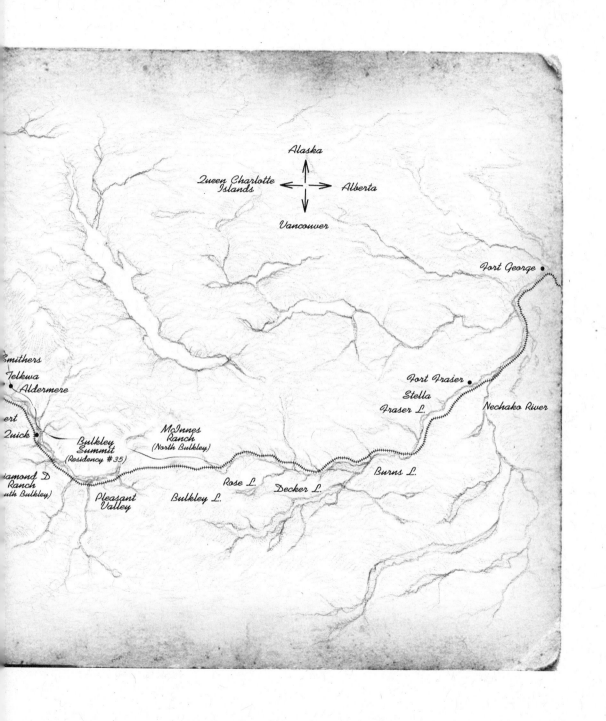

Passengers enjoy the first passenger train out of Prince Rupert to the end of steel, 1911. At this time the end of steel, the end of the track, was west of Kitselas Canyon. It took a full day to cover just under one hundred miles. *Bulkley Valley Museum, P0500*

NOTE FROM THE AUTHOR

I have, with respect, gently rearranged Bernice's reminiscences. For clarity, I have corrected her punctuation. I have not corrected spelling errors in her letters, choosing instead to let them be as she originally wrote them. With thorough archival research I have corrected place names and the names of railway employees when I could confirm an error. I have, with restraint, omitted repeated stories. The complete letters of Bernice Medbury Martin, in their original state, reside in the provincial archives in Victoria and the Bulkley Valley Museum in Smithers.

Bernice Medbury Martin stands outside a typical temporary GTP camp building holding her dinner, a grouse and a fish. Temporary camps were set up all along the line to house and feed labourers, store railway equipment and camp supplies. *Bulkley Valley Museum, P 534*

RIGHT: Bernice Medbury Martin holding kittens at her home in Decker Lake. *Bulkley Valley Museum, P2843*

BEGINNINGS

Bernice Medbury was born in October 1882 in Fond du Lac, Wisconsin. Her mother was Eunice Eastman and her father Chauncey Medbury, a travelling salesman turned successful entrepreneur. Chauncey was one of the founders of Gurney Refrigeration Company, which made the bold step in 1891 to manufacture and sell a small refrigerator designed especially for use in the home. Bernice had an older sister Ruth, a younger sister Marjorie and a younger brother Chauncey Jr.

Bernice attended elementary school in Fond du Lac and then enrolled in Oshkosh Normal School for "young ladies and gentlemen." She went on to study at the Pratt Institute in New York.

On February 14, 1912, at the age of thirty, Bernice Medbury married Leslie Frank Martin in an evening ceremony at her family home in Fond du Lac, Wisconsin.

Leslie Martin was also from Fond du Lac. His widowed mother was Mrs. H.E. Martin and he had one brother named Art. Leslie was a railroader and at the time of his marriage to Bernice was working on the construction of the Grand Trunk Pacific Railway (GTPR) in northern British Columbia. Leslie worked as the bookkeeper on a large grade clearing and levelling camp on the Skeena River run by subcontractor Donald A. Rankin.

Leslie Frank Martin, winter 1912.
Bulkley Valley Museum, P528

Immediately following their celebration, newlyweds Leslie and Bernice bid farewell to their families in Fond du Lac and headed to Seattle, Washington. From there they travelled by steamer to Vancouver, British Columbia. From Vancouver, Bernice and Leslie journeyed north 575 nautical miles (1,065 nautical kilometres) aboard a steamer along the wild BC coastline. They arrived at the rising pioneer city of Prince Rupert at the end of February 1912.

Bernice was immediately enamoured with northern British Columbia and richly described the camp life, the extreme weather, her various homes and the many colourful characters she encountered in letters to her mother, father, sisters and brother back in Wisconsin. She wrote one letter to her cousin Vivian who also lived in Fond du Lac.

The Grand Trunk Pacific Railway

In the early nineteen hundreds, Kaien Island, a small island off the northern Pacific coast of British Columbia, was the focus of much speculation and surveying. A large party made up of harbour engineers, surveyors, carpenters, an accountant, a stenographer and a draftsman entered Tuck Inlet on Kaien Island and proceeded to survey, map and stake out the proposed city of Prince Rupert and the wharf facilities for the Grand Trunk Pacific Railway.

While harbour engineers cut through thick coastal brush and laid out the port facility at Prince Rupert, GTPR company representatives lobbied the provincial and federal governments and the British Crown to support their transcontinental railway.

The newly established port city of Prince Rupert was the northern arrival point for many railroaders and pioneers who came in on the coastal steamers. Bernice arrived in Prince Rupert in 1912 as stores were being built, streets were being laid out and settlers were clamouring for a start on the steep-sided community. Bernice was accompanied by her husband Leslie who was returning to a railroad construction camp 112 miles up the Skeena River. *Bulkley Valley Museum, P1906*

Steady rain caused surveyors' tents to leak, as GTPR engineers decided on a superior standard for the construction of the Grand Trunk Pacific, and while men worked in their gumboots by day and slept in their gumboots at night, company president Charles Melville Hays stood in boardrooms in England and expounded on the virtues of his Grand Trunk Pacific Railway.

Charles Melville Hays spoke persuasively about the high volumes of traffic he was certain would use his proposed northern transcontinental and he convinced the federal government that they would easily recover the cost of construction. In 1903 Prime Minister Wilfred Laurier and his federal Liberal government entered into an agreement with GTPR to build a northern railway route across the prairies and to the Pacific coast. The eastern part of the railway, from Winnipeg, Manitoba, to Moncton,

The construction of the Grand Trunk Pacific Railway was an enormous undertaking. All of the construction materials and equipment, the ditchers, steam shovels and thousands of tons of steel rails, were shipped to Prince Rupert and then stockpiled on the docks. *Bulkley Valley Museum, P1479*

New Brunswick, would be built by the federal government. The western part, the 1,756 miles (2,826 kilometres) from Winnipeg, Manitoba, to Prince Rupert, British Columbia, would be built by the federally supported and British-based Grand Trunk Pacific Railway.

In 1905, railway construction began moving westward from Winnipeg. By 1907, the land at Prince Rupert was being cleared and a small sawmill enabled the construction of shacks on stilts and planks. A year later, steel was shipped by steamer to the newly established port of Prince Rupert and construction on the Grand Trunk Pacific Railway began eastward along the north side of the Skeena River.

In the spring of 1909 Prince Rupert lots went on sale to a frenzy of speculative bidders. In September 1909, the Prince Rupert *Optimist* newspaper stated: "...the population is three thousand and the building is spreading over the townsite in a wonderful manner. We now have a newspaper and job office, one butcher shop and two drugstores, twenty-five real estate agencies, four grocery stores, two laundries, one millinery parlour, fourteen restaurants, two hardware stores, two furniture stores, one theatre, one fancy goods store, one clothing store, one bakery, three barristers, three barbers, two coal merchants and three lumberyards."

Many hundreds of people came to northern British Columbia, arriving by coastal steamer to Prince Rupert or overland from Quesnel and Fort George, to work on the construction of the "Mountain Section" of the GTPR. Labourers found working conditions rugged and the wages low. The "Wild West" of northern British Columbia proved too remote and many hundreds of workers and settlers left. But for every person leaving there were more arriving and the newly established towns were settled with brave and optimistic populations. Retailers and investors came North and during these years of railway construction there was a boom in mining and agricultural activity.

The Grand Trunk Pacific Railway was built with a superior grade and easy curves, with steel and concrete bridges over major crossings and heavier-than-usual railway

Hundreds of tons of earth, clay, mud and rocks were moved to build the rail grade. Huge shovels powered by steam were used to try to save labour costs and speed up the pace of construction. But the heavy machinery often sank in the mud or was buried in slides and it was the labourers who then had to dig and haul the steam shovels out. *Bulkley Valley Museum, P0521*

ties. The chosen route of the railway was unusually challenging. Three thousand tons of powder was used in the first hundred miles alone, between Prince Rupert and Kitselas Canyon. The track was built from coastal Prince Rupert inland along the north side of the Skeena River, crossing to the south side of the Skeena, following the Bulkley River to the its source near Decker Lake and then pushing farther inland to Fraser Lake. The railway right-of-way clearing and track laying penetrated through vast wilderness, which was sparsely populated, over fluctuating major river systems and alongside, and in some cases right through, massive mountain ranges. A separate team of railroaders was building westward from Alberta, over the Rocky Mountains, through Fort George and farther westward to meet the eastward laying team near Fraser Lake.

In 1914, after six years of difficult construction eastward from Prince Rupert, the Grand Trunk Pacific Railway was completed when the track-laying team from the west met the track-laying team from the east at Fort Fraser near Fraser Lake, 375 miles (604 kilometres) inland from Prince Rupert.

At a staggering cost of $112,000 per mile, the Grand Trunk Pacific Railway fulfilled its promise to build a railway through northern British Columbia that connected the newly established towns and the resources of the North with the rest of Canada. The cost per mile was extraordinarily high but the Grand Trunk Pacific was not just an average railway built over usual terrain.

Due to World War I the predicted rail traffic was never realized, nor was the increased population in the northern towns and cities. Splendidly built but under-utilized, the Grand Trunk Pacific Railway was severely in debt, cut off from investors and suffering from low rail traffic. In 1918 the federal government took over the GTPR and formed a crown corporation, Canadian National Railways (CNR).

The scenic route of the Grand Trunk Pacific Railway is travelled today by a passenger service that boasts a pleasant ride and offers glimpses at the still "Wild West" of northern British Columbia. Passengers in the viewing car can see the 1913 date etched into the entrances of the frequent tunnels. Freight trains also travel the former GTPR route with long lines of container shipments to and from the port of Prince Rupert, still closer to Asian markets than the port of Vancouver.

WINTER 1912

"The roadbed tilted so much that the boxcars would tip."

At the time of Bernice and Leslie's arrival Prince Rupert was a community thriving because of the Grand Trunk Pacific Railway. Construction on the railway began in 1908 and the docks at Prince Rupert were continually replenished with stockpiles of railway ties and equipment needed to build the railway pushing eastward along the north side of the Skeena River.

Charles Melville Hays had petitioned the Canadian federal Liberals to build a second transcontinental railway through the northern part of British Columbia. Hays had stated that a railway through northern BC would stimulate economic growth and, for Prince Rupert in 1912, he was right. The steep streets of Prince Rupert were busy with entrepreneurial merchants, coastal and interior First Nations and hundreds of railway labourers. Hardy miners, pioneer settlers and zealous missionaries were

ABOVE: The track-laying crew worked hard and fast, throwing down wooden ties and spiking the heavy steel rails in place as soon as they were lowered down. No contractor wanted to make Dan Dempsey's track-laying team wait and every effort was made to finish clearing and levelling the rail grade before the Pioneer arrived. *The Fraser Fort George Museum Society and the Exploration Place, P981-9-121*

coming and going from points inland. Prince Rupert's inhabitants numbered 4,184 in 1912, with hundreds more roving through the port city with the arrivals and departures of the steamers to and from the southern cities of Vancouver, Victoria and Seattle.

Leslie returned with his bride at the height of railway construction. By January 1912 hundreds of labourers had slashed and burned the right-of-way, blasted stumps and rocks, cut through rocky mountainsides and filled in gaps and gullies (with shovels and wheelbarrows) to build the rail grade and lay track 80 miles (129 kilometres) up the Skeena River. In February there were 1,277 men working on the west end of railway construction, and the tracks had been laid up to Kitselas Canyon where hundreds of men worked on building four tunnels.

The railroaders worked twelve months of the year in all kinds of extreme northern weather and through very difficult terrain. Contractors moved men and supplies inland using the Skeena River or the newly laid railway to camps stationed anywhere from three to fifteen miles (five to twenty-four kilometres) apart. Food and shelter and even medical services varied according to which sub-

Foley, Welch & Stewart

Together Timothy Foley, Patrick Welch and John W. Stewart made up the railway-building firm of Foley, Welch and Stewart. FWS was the principal contractor for the mountain section of the Grand Trunk Pacific Railway. The firm hired and paid subcontractors to do the grading and building of the railway and implemented a cost-plus system. Workers along the line referred to the additional 5 percent that FWS charged as the "kiss of death" for the subcontractor.

As individual businessmen, Foley, Welch and Stewart invested in mines near Hazelton and Telkwa and in southern British Columbia. Their firm was also involved in other railway projects as well as the building of the Welland Canal in Ontario and construction of the Halifax Harbour.

Foley, Welch and Stewart have peaks named after them in the Cheam Range in the Yale Land District, east of Chilliwack, BC.

The proximity of the railway to the Skeena River made the GTPR very difficult to build. The rail grade was often washed away or undercut by fluctuating river levels. The newly cleared and levelled rail grade awaits the tracklayer. *Prince Rupert City and Regional Archives and the Museum of Northern BC, JRW128 (WP 997-107-14132)*

contractor was in charge of the camp and how financially supported he was by Foley, Welch and Stewart, the main contractors for the Grand Trunk Pacific Railway.

The railway was built eastward alongside the temperamental Skeena River and the pace of construction was subject to fluctuating water levels as the snowpack in the mountains melted and ran out into creeks and streams and joined the river. As it neared its Pacific Ocean outflow, the Skeena River's water levels were also affected by tidal currents.

Under the watchful eye of the Grand Trunk Pacific residency engineers the track was built with very high standards. It boasts gentle, wide curves, a slowly rising and falling track grade, heavy rails and superiorly constructed crossings. The GTPR chose heavy eighty-pound (thirty-six-kilogram) rails, instead of the usual sixty-five-pound (twenty-nine-kilogram) standard and used concrete and steel on all major crossing bridges. Such high standards led to difficult working conditions, slower construction and unusually high expenses.

Steel had passed through the railway town of Van Arsdol just downstream from Kitselas Canyon and was advancing every day towards Skeena Crossing, the long bridge that crossed the Skeena River 165 miles (266 kilometres) inland from Prince Rupert. The trains that ran were rarely on schedule due to bridge washouts, tunnel cave-ins or slides. In the winter of 1912 the slow-moving mixed trains carried railroaders, construction materials, camp supplies and cramped passengers who were forced to disembark at the last station along the new line as the work train rumbled on to the end of steel. Passenger service was not comfortable and complaints were fre-

Kitselas, on the south side of the Skeena River. Hundreds of railroad labourers frequently left their construction camps on the north side and crossed the Skeena River on the ice or by ferry to Kitselas. The temporary boom town boasted stores, a newspaper office, rooming houses, restaurants and a hotel with the one coveted liquor licence. *Prince Rupert City and Regional Archives and the Museum of Northern BC, JRWPA 95014*

quently reported in the area newspapers; one printed the complaint that, "the carriage of ties, rails and supplies prevents the giving of anything like passenger service."

To reach their destinations beyond the end of the tracks, people walked. If they could afford the fares they could go along with one of the many freighters moving supplies farther inland. During the winter of 1912 heavily loaded dog teams mushed from end of steel along the frozen Skeena River to Hazelton. There were so many dog teams that residents of Prince Rupert complained of dogs being stolen from yards by the Hazelton mushers. A popular winter ride and reliable freighter was the *Skeena River Mail and Express*, a horse-drawn sleigh operated by Hazelton men George Beirnes and Barney Mulvaney.

During construction of the GTPR horse-drawn stages were very busy hauling passengers and freight from the end of steel to inland pioneer towns. This stage used the frozen Skeena River as its route. *Prince Rupert City and Regional Archives and the Museum of Northern BC, WP 1998-062-17276*

Hardscrabble was a temporary camp 112 miles (180 kilometres) inland from Prince Rupert on the north side of the Skeena River, twelve miles (nineteen kilometres) above Kitselas Canyon. Leslie had lived at D.A. Rankin's Camp 22, Hardscrabble, since 1911 and worked as bookkeeper of the nearby construction. Hardscrabble was a hub of railroader activity located near the newly laid tracks of the GTPR, established only to house and feed the construction men and store the contractors' supplies. Those living at Hardscrabble would venture westward down the tracks either to the railway community of Newtown, officially named Van Arsdol, or south across the Skeena River to the pioneer community of Kitselas to gather their mail and socialize.

Kitselas was originally a stopping spot for the sternwheelers before they headed up through the Skeena River's narrow and rocky Kitselas Canyon. In 1907 the BC Voters List had only seven names from this community; most listed themselves as miners or farmers. In 1910 the railroad construction was across the river from the community of Kitselas, 100 miles (161 kilometres) inland from Prince Rupert. Despite being on the opposite side of the river, Kitselas became a popular railroader's town. Railroaders would cross from their work sites on the north side of the Skeena to the south side, reaching Kitselas over the ice in winter or by a ferry in warmer months. Many hundreds of men worked day and night on the four tunnels—three of which measured 400, 700 and 1,100 feet (122, 213, 335 metres) long—located downstream from Kitselas Canyon. Merchants moved in and Kitselas grew to have one rooming house, two hotels (one with a liquor licence), two general stores and a poolroom. In the boom of construction there were times when the bar take at the end of the night was one thousand dollars—this at a time when men earned $2.50 to $2.75 a day.

On the north or railway-track side of the Skeena River was a railroader's camp, a community known to locals as Newtown but officially a station stop named Van Arsdol for Grand Trunk Pacific divisional engineer C.C. Van Arsdol. The rail town of Van Arsdol operated as headquarters for all the supplies and the many hundreds of men working at blasting tunnels.

Despite the snow and freezing temperatures the rails progressed along the Skeena River and through the tunnels, through Van Arsdol, through Leslie's camp at Hardscrabble and on to John Bostrom's cut contract at Mile 151. Bernice was literally at the centre of construction, witnessing the building of a railway right beside their small cabin at Hardscrabble. Leslie and Bernice lived at Hardscrabble for the rest of the winter as the work progressed up the Skeena River. As bookkeeper, Leslie was one of the last men to leave Camp 22; he had to wait for the camp to be closed before he could gather all records and finish up his books.

As the work progressed up the Skeena River, contractors Foley, Welch and Stewart moved ahead of the labourers and established a large freight depot at Captain McLeod's camp near the site of the Skeena Crossing Bridge 165 miles (266 kilometres) inland from Prince Rupert.

As winter let loose its grip on Northerners, in March 1912, the steel was being laid to the north side of the Skeena Crossing Bridge. Contracts on the north side of the Skeena were completed and subcontractors looked to the Interior for their next contract. Railroaders organized the transportation of their narrow track, steam shovels and dump cars, their wheelbarrow, picks and shovels; scores of railroad labourers picked up what was theirs, abandoned the camps and moved inland.

~

PRINCE RUPERT, BC
FEBRUARY 27, 1912

Dearest family,
Got in to Prince Rupert. Glorious sunshiny day with hoarfrost over everything. Leslie and I were met at the boat with rice.

Les knows everyone here, at least everyone not a bohunk is someone, a contractor or engineer or some sort. We got into town and the entire male population was out to see us in. Both Mrs. Parker and Mrs. Orme were there to meet us. We went up to Parker's, a three-room shack right near town. Mr. Parker, Stan, is Les's

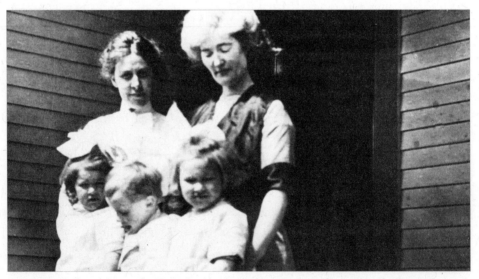

Bernice was welcomed to northern British Columbia by her new Prince Rupert friends, Mrs. Parker (right) and Mrs. Bowness (left) and their children Francis and Margaret Bowness and little Jimmie Parker.
Bulkley Valley Museum, P2848

Kyote Blasting Method

Professional Engineer John Strickland Leitch worked on the GTPR construction out of Prince Rupert between 1908 and 1910. Here Mr. Leitch explains the blasting system that was used:

The efficient rock men were Swedes, Norwegians and Finns. In those days there were no compressors or power drills. It was all handwork and it was quite common for a drill gang of two hammer men and a drill handler to put down twenty feet in one day. The blasted rock was all loaded by hand on flat dump cars and gin pole derricks powered by horses.

The kyote system of blasting consisted of driving a small tunnel, just large enough for a man to kneel or sit in, in the face of the cliff about one foot below grade elevation, to about the inner side of the cut. Then drifting would be made for forty to fifty feet each way along the line where the road ditch would come. We of the engineering party had to give the tunnellers the levels and reference points and make checks of alignment of the entrance tunnels and lateral drifts. This work was all hand drilling and blasting and a lot of

A large blast goes off on the north side of the Skeena River above a sternwheeler landing site.
Bulkley Valley Museum, P0203

continued...

it was by candle and lantern light with no power fans to clear away the fumes after blasting. It was hard, tedious and slow work and one had to admire the skilful men who had the courage and stamina to carry it through. We had several cuts where it took from five to six months to complete the tunnel and drift work for these kyote blasts. These holes were loaded with a combination of 40 percent dynamite and black blasting powder. It took workmen several days to load and tamp these kyote holes and often as much as twenty tons of explosives were used in a single blast. An explosion was fired at a safe distance by a blaster employing a battery trigger mechanism. It was most interesting to watch these blasts since often a huge slice of rock would be ripped off the side of a cliff. The blasting cut ran many times over a hundred feet up the rock face. Then the lower face would be pushed out in a mass of very large jagged boulders. Quite a large quantity of rock was blown into the Skeena River but a large part remained where it could be used as fill.

⌐

The drill team Leitch refers to consisted of a drill handler who kept a firm grip on the bar and twisted it while trying to stay clear of the two hammer men who took turns smashing the long bar into the rocks.

business partner. Mrs. Parker is good looking, simple and quite substantial. She was rather afraid that the bride would scorn her simple mode of living. I did not. I like her and made friends with little Jimmie so I got on first rate.

Happy, well and bushels of love,

Bernice

⌐

BROWN'S CAMP AT VAN ARSDOL, GTPRR BC, MILE 100
FRIDAY, MARCH 1, 1912

My dear Marjorie,
Wednesday at noon we scrambled aboard the train leaving Prince Rupert. All the laundry would not go in anywhere so we put it in my blue hat bag and started with it in our hand.

Labour Divisions

Many thousands of wooden railway ties were needed for the construction and maintenance of the Grand Trunk Pacific Railway. Using the stands of timber close to the line of construction, hundreds of men found work as tie cutters. "The tie cutting was done by French Canadians and brawny Finlanders, considered by most to be the most expert axemen in existence," wrote Walter Wicks in *Memories of the Skeena*.

Generally, Scandinavians did much of the blasting and tunnelling for the construction of the Grand Trunk Pacific Railway, especially along the Skeena River. Pioneer W.J. "Wiggs" O'Neill referred to these men as talented hardrock men.

Despite a 1908 agreement between the provincial government and the Grand Trunk Pacific Railway, which stated that for the construction of the railway within BC "white labour shall be exclusively employed unless permitted by the Lieutenant-Governor," Chinese and Japanese workers still found employment clearing Kaien Island for

Charlie, New Hazelton. *Bulkley Valley Museum, P0879*

the city of Prince Rupert and at construction camps along the line as cooks, laundry workers and occasionally as general labourers. These few brave workers were referred to disparagingly as "chinks."

"Nearly all the timekeepers and bookkeepers on the job were Scotchmen," wrote O'Neill in *Steamboat Days of the Skeena*. "The management [Foley,

continued...

Welch and Stewart] of course was pretty clannish." Leslie Martin, book-keeper, identified himself on the 1911 census at Camp 22, Hardscrabble, as an American of Scotch heritage.

W.J. "Wiggs" O'Neill also reminisced that, "the Italians and Montenegrins did the earthwork;" that is, the back-breaking digging, filling and hauling of the earth, the clay and the gumbo.

The 1911 census, which included the tie cutting and railway camps along the Skeena River, shows that hundreds of the young, single men identified themselves as Montenegrin. In Bernice's letters these hard-working eastern European labourers were derisively referred to as "bohunks."

As Walter Wicks wrote, "Not many of these foreign workers returned to their motherland. Many settled in their adopted country. Their children and grandchildren are here to stay."

I set it on the platform and some way it got knocked off and rolled under the platform. A large fat man followed it, rolling under and picked it up, a Mr. MacArthur.

It is only 100 miles, takes several hours and the scenery is beautiful. The train is full of bohunks and plenty of excitement. Just outside of Prince Rupert at a crossing over the Skeena we were held up for hours. The bridge was open to put in the first concrete pier. They had been working all night but the derrick had broken and we just had to wait.

We walked up past the length of the train to see the works then back to see the camp. Saw two of the Indian canoes then back down the railway track to see a lovely waterfall and the mouth of the tunnel we had just come through. Loads of people came up on the train as this is the last passenger stop.

I love the country, find the people lovely and have quite concluded I shall fit in and be very happy. Leslie is so well known, respected and happy, has so much decision and go that it is a delight to see him. We are so happy together and I love him better every day. He says I am a game sport because I don't kick at a thing. I wonder what he expected me to do?

The trains here are tri-weekly and the boats too so the mails go slowly. All our mail should go to Kitselas, Box 38.

Most things are the same as at home. Money is only different in that there are no pennies and they have little silver nickels and Canadian quarters.

Les ordered a crate of oranges and apples and some vegetables and fruit the camp does not afford. We had to buy a crate of eggs, 30 dozen for some dollars, we will share this with camp.

[Les has gone ahead, up the tracks to Hardscrabble.] Tonight I go up to Les on the engine of a freight train. I must be ready when the train comes.

I am as happy as a clam. You must not miss me with that lump in your throat feeling at all. Just think of how I love you and you love me.

Your little Bernice

NEWTOWN, BC
SATURDAY, MARCH 2, 1912
AL BROWN'S WIFE'S CABIN

My dear family,
Saturday evening and the tri-weekly train is just in.

This is mile 100 of the Grand Trunk Pacific Railroad. The last station to which tickets are sold. End of steel is way up beyond Hardscrabble and advancing every day. From there to Hazelton Barney Mulvaney runs a stage for passengers and a dog team.

Foley, Welch and Stewart have a steamboat office here. Al Brown is the head of the steamboat office and Frank Bowness runs a bunkhouse and eating camp.

Mrs. Brown has a nice cabin with a living room and two bedrooms. We are her guests and eat at the cook shanty. They have a splendid Chinese cook and boy.

From Prince Rupert all the way up the mark of the railroad is apparent. We go back down to the bay right on the water's edge for a couple of miles, dry dock over riverboats, wireless station across the island, quarantine over beyond, an Indian village and Port Essington on islands. On the edge of the RR right-of-way are various canneries. Then we turn in and follow the Skeena River, which is wide and rapid.

Dan Dempsey and his team of men laid track from Prince Rupert eastward. This photo was taken from the flatcar of the tracklayer which held wooden railway ties until they were shunted forward for track building. This tracklayer is working its way from the Kitselas tunnels toward Skeena Crossing, January 1912. *Prince Rupert City and Regional Archives and the Museum of Northern BC, JRW451*

Trees covered with hoar frost, and snow capped mountains all the way.

At about 40 miles is Archie McDougall's tunnel. The original roadbed was around a mountain but the snow and landslides smashed the snow shed so they burrowed through. Every few miles was someone's old camp, so and so fill or cut. Now the camps are in disuse, little new yellow stations are all fixed up and the RR sells regular tickets to the stations. There was a bridge across an inlet that took two years to build and one minute to cross. There is slack water only 15 minutes in 24 hours.

It took us till 8 pm to get to the Browns'. Al and Mrs. Brown met us at the track and we walked over a few steps to this place. He is short, fat and dark with plenty of force despite lack of chin and she is Maria Mae in color and get up. They both grow nicer all the time and have taken me right in.

Tunnelling

Professional Engineer John Strickland Leitch explains tunnelling:

The tunnelling was all manual work. Fortunately for the progress of the project the men were all experts. In those early pioneering days of tunnel work there were no electric lights or ventilating fans. The only lighting source was lanterns. For ventilation and clearing of the dynamite fumes a tight wooden box duct about two feet square was carried along the top of the heading and one of similar size was placed along at grade level. They were built in sixteen-foot sections and erected in place as the work advanced. It was really surprising how well this ventilating system worked and it was a great time saver as the men could resume work soon after blasting. The main section of the tunnel was excavated by drilling holes to a foot below the grade level. The workmen did an excellent job of driving twenty-foot wide tunnels through that igneous red granite and it was really surprising how precisely they followed the dimensions of the tunnel cross-section: there was very little overbreak in

KITSELAS TUNNEL G.T.P.R. SKEENA RIVER. BC

Construction of the four tunnels skirting Kitselas Canyon took hundreds of men two years to complete. In February of 1911, when Leslie Martin was living and working in camp east of Kitselas, five men were killed, two severely injured and eight more narrowly escaped when a box of dynamite exploded at the mouth of one of the Kitselas tunnels. *Prince Rupert City and Regional Archives and the Museum of Northern BC, JRWPA 95446*

the entire length. Although the mountainside which the tunnel pierced was rough and rugged we managed to lay out the centre line very carefully on the ground. On the curve we had to give centre line points quite often.

Friday I walked a little and had tea with Mrs. Ross next door. She keeps house for her son Harris in a three-room shack and serves tea with all the charm and good taste a wonderful woman and a lovely service could impart. Today I ironed over at the cook shanty and at 4 Les wired that he was walking in. Mrs. Brown and I started to meet him. We met Les just at the curve where we see the "Seven Sisters" across the river, seven snow tipped mountains.

At sunset we look up the track, see a mountain covered with hoar frosted evergreen trees, lavender in the sunset with pink snow against robin-egg blue sky.

At our left the woods, at our right the river roaring down despite being almost icebound. There is the most gorgeous moonlight. I am drinking it in as fast as I can and some time I will get so charged with it that it will overflow and you will get the benefit.

Leslie says our cabin is alright and we go up the tracks tomorrow and back with our chattels and then I shall see my new home. Bushels of little things to say, those that come a hundred times a day. Everything is nicer than I thought it would be.

Bernice

HARDSCRABBLE, BC
CAMP 22, MILE 112
THURSDAY, MARCH 14, 1912

My dear family,

When I tell you about the roadbed here you will understand something of what this traveling is like. Up here, where the train stopped to let me off the night I came, the snow was shovelled off, the ties dumped out and the rails spiked down. The roadbed tilted so much they were such the boxcars would tip. They tucked some cordwood, kitchen stove sized, under the ties on the down end. Some places the ties are together, some places a lady's step apart, some places a man's step and some (woe is me) are farther than my jumping distance in my blue skirt.

Al Brown had wired in and secured a permit for me to ride from Van Arsdol up to Hardscrabble. Van Arsdol is the last stop for passengers and past Van Arsdol the road is so bad only construction trains run and they go off the track a dozen times a run so permit to ride is quite essential.

When the long freight drew up the caboose stopped outside the office. The conductor leaned out of the cupola and howled at Brown, "The next time I stop my train at your old office for a passenger…" Much scorn! My coat, a big bag, a box of candy and my straw hat resting on a large fresh green cabbage and a Saturday *Seattle Times* and I scuttled onto the train with the aid of Bowness and Brown while Mrs. Brown and Mrs. Orme stood outside and waved me on.

It was about 9 o'clock; inside the caboose supper was just being cleared and one man asleep on his cot. As the train started a large man descended from the cupola and strode over to me a paper in his hand, "Mrs. Martin will you please sign this." I read it through, "Mrs. Leslie Martin hereby releases the GTPRR from liability in case of accident while she is riding in the construction train." I signed it and tried to smile pleasantly. When he put the paper up he turned his sunny morning face toward me and invited me up in his sky parlour to see the sights.

There was no moon but we could see a little. Inside of a mile the caboose struck a snag. The conductor released the air brake and the train stopped and the brakeman disappeared like magic. There was only a boulder under the train so we moved on in the dark. The conductor talked all the way up and told me about the cuts, the tunnels (four of which we went through) and fills. He told me about the Kitselas rapids and big canyon. We crept along one and a half hours to go twelve miles. The next day when I saw the road and I was not surprised.

We stopped at the road beside the steam shovel and there was Leslie. Gee, I was glad to see him. He shouldered my duds and off we trailed in the dark up a trail into the woods. The snow had a lovely crust and so we walked on and on by the light of a bobbing lantern. Presently we passed a cabin and then came to our own. Leslie hung the lantern and I had my first view of my new home.

There were grand logs the length of the cabin for ceiling beams. Side walls wainscoted about three feet with nice lumber. The bed is high. The little table and chairs were all out and sitting around sociable like and there was a nice fire in the airtight heater. The kitchen is nice and roomy and was full of "just moved in." Both doors of the cabin will just let me walk through with my head up, Leslie has to bow or bump. He often bumps.

Camp Life

Thousands of transient men lived in the temporary railway camps but only a few wrote about their experiences. Walter Wicks in his book *Memories of the Skeena* was one man who recalled the camps on the lower Skeena:

The water was sluiced into camp by a wooden trough and any kind of barrel or box or hole dug in the ground contained our water supply. Each camp was built of rough lumber boards and we used the traditional outhouse since no metal plumbing was ever in sight. Workers' accident and health agencies were never in existence on the country's largest construction project. Men washed their clothing and themselves in a wash basin, and felt lucky to have one. Food was delivered to camp mostly by river paddlewheelers. Fresh vegetables were always short, fresh fruit more so. The cookhouse menu was fair and not so fair depending on the cook, the contractor and the buying agent.

W.J. "Wiggs" O'Neill freighted supplies to Skeena River camps and

A camp at the temporary community of Bateman's Landing, near present-day Terrace. A group of Grand Trunk Pacific men stand outside Dr. Johns's medical building. Dr. Johns used the dogs to transport medical supplies upriver. *Bulkley Valley Museum, P0202*

recalled, "...the most disgraceful set-up in the contractors operation was their hospital arrangement on the work... along the line the odd board shack was made of rough boards, with nothing in them, and absolutely no equipment."

The tough conditions at the railway camps led to Foley, Welch and Stewart's nickname, Fool 'em, Work 'em and Starve 'em.

My front yard view is 25 ft wide then another 29 down then you see the frozen river. It is about twice as wide as our house and then up go the mountains. Some evergreen trees on the mountainside in spite of the rock but no mortal or goat could hang on.

I love it here. I wear my sweater over my gingham dress and no need for warmer clothes.

Good night, best love, and don't be sorry for me,

Bernice

⟷

March 25, 1912
Hardscrabble, BC

My dear Marjorie,

Your letter came and consumed nearly a forenoon. Oh, it was a delight. Right now let me say that I am not off this earth at all. I am just the same person. I do and think and eat and sleep and wake and do and live just the same as before I came here.

You see the train goes down from Newtown three times a week. Our letters go to Kitselas whenever anyone is going. This is Monday and I am out in front of the cottage on a pile of lumber. My back is to the sun while I am writing and I enjoy the fresh air and the bird songs. To continue—supposing the letter gets to Kitselas. Then it takes the first boat handy, Tuesday night, Thursday, Friday or Saturday. I get to the mailing point about twenty minutes late each every time.

Last Sunday, St. Patrick's Day, we had the first bad weather since I have been here; a wet snow. Les had been to Newtown. Al Brown came up and met him by handcar the night before. He got home about 9:30 and said he had bought a speeder. A RR three-cornered thing that will carry two people and some luggage on the railway tracks. I was so pleased.

On Sunday we arose early, breakfasted on waffles and I picked up the house. Then we read and soon it stopped snowing. About three we started over the cut to get on the speeder and went down to camp.

At Camp 22, Harry Rankin is the timekeeper on the work, Snell is the steam shovel man and Les is the boss. D.A. Rankin never stopped here. Harry Rankin and Cunningham, the Dominion Government Telegraph operator, live in the commissary.

We went to the engineers little office with two bedrooms behind. There is a bunkhouse for the helpers and cookhouse to cook and eat and for the chink to live in. Bruce Lillico, a nice, cheery, good-looking, well-mannered chap, rather out of sort, invited us to stay for tea. We did.

Dinner or tea with enamel or granite cups and plates, steel knives and forks. Most of the food served in tin dishes with horrid iron spoons and they all suggest as though it were a sterilized balanced ration.

———

Back for a quiet evening by ourselves.

Leslie had to go up along the Skeena River to the construction site at Skeena Crossing. Perhaps it will be a three day trip so he was off for Newtown to arrange to get Mrs. Brown to stay with me as previously arranged. I scuttled that day—swept, ironed, cleaned lamps, baked bread, curled my hair (a kingdom for a curling iron). At 7:30, as dark was closing in, I started for the cut with my lantern. I met Mrs. Brown and Les half way in. Leslie slept on our cot couch bed and Mrs. B and I slept in the bed.

The next day Les did not get the train at all. You see this is above the scheduled runs and no one knows when the train will be back and forth.

We went to camp for excitement and the fresh roast. Saw a shovel working and two small shots in blast.

The next morning I heard the train whistle at 7:45. Les jumped into his boots, I held a cup of coffee under his nose and handed him a biscuit and he started to run. He had to get some papers into camp and get back to the train. Luckily it was the up train he wanted for that one we hear a whistle for a long way off. The river is so walled-in it carries this way. He was gone till Saturday afternoon.

We girls visited and slept, sewed, washed dishes and Saturday I washed the floor. Don't worry in spite of soft coal, Tony the dog, Tony the Italian [one of the many transient characters about camp] and Leslie and my boots, I don't scrub that often, just where the effect will most attract the eye. We made curtains for the wardrobe, three lengths of cheesecloth with three large nails apiece for weights. Mrs. Brown made curtains for the

The *Inlander* going through Kitselas Canyon. This sternwheeler was one of many operating on the Skeena River during construction of the Grand Trunk Pacific Railway. Kitselas Canyon was a narrow, rocky section of swift water that was responsible for numerous wrecks and fatalities. *Bulkley Valley Museum, P1911*

doorway, hemmed at the top with little brass rings to slip on a rod of bale wire.

Saturday evening at seven we three and two grips started for Newtown on the speeder. I sat opposite Leslie and pumped for about three miles when we saw a light ahead. When I could only distinguish a man with a lantern, Leslie said, "Taylor, the donkey engine man. We will take him aboard if you two girls can ride together." We did somehow. It was dark and the little new moon for light. We were stopping just before the big tunnel to be sure there was no train coming when lo and behold there was. Oh you scramble. Mrs. Brown and I grabbed the bags and the men the speeder. Les said, "Now you girls get back we have no time to run this speeder in and I don't want to get jumped. This is Dan Dempsey's train." We sat on a log and ostriched our faces behind Mrs. Brown's muff. Well, the train swept mysteriously by. Leslie and Taylor counted out all the men they knew and really had time to shake hands if they

Thousands of men worked long hours building the railway. Here labourers hitch a ride to their next camp on a flatcar along a newly completed section of track.

Work conditions were tough and wages were low. For every two men arriving there were two leaving.
Prince Rupert City and Regional Archives and the Museum of Northern BC, WP997-107-14133

so desired. It was an enormous work train going up to Skeena Crossing.

Then we hopped on our speeder and went merrily along. The train was past but just through the third tunnel we saw a light. It proved to be a bohunkie railway worker. He had built a fire out of chips and we stopped to warm our toes. We were then just across from Kitselas and at the same time on the lower end of the big canyon. At present people cross on the ice, later they will cross by ferry boat. As we neared Newtown there were three engines in view, the regular train, Saturday night was a double header and a freight switcher from the yard in Littleton.

It was pitch-dark. Coming along the track were big men with packs. They were going ahead to steal a ride as the train came up or to walk to Kitselas. You see the train carries no one without permits from that point on they are all ordered off the train. It is at their own risk that they sneak on when the train is in motion.

We stayed all night and helped the Browns off for town [Prince Rupert] in the morning. Mr. Brown looked quite like a regular man in his street clothes. The ones he wears on the work are a sight. He looks like a fat young bear. Leslie in his high water is a dude beside Al. I find Les is quite a dude at that.

—

Here I sit at 12:30 in the sunshine. My coat off, my yarn cap on my head and rubber boots on my feet. It is thawing today and these slip on faster than the lace up boots. I walk out to the track with Les every day, sometimes twice. At four I start to camp to walk back with him and pick up some meat for dinner.

Oh, so much to say. Our food, our cottage house, how well we are and how easily we have grown used to each other. And how gradually our little cabin is becoming a home and, aye, even I with a million dollar education, have made some housekeeper.

We got some nuts, raisins and a cabbage. You see the stores for all five riverboats are kept there. Before long the whole affair is to be moved to Skeena Crossing and none of the boats will compete with the RR in this part of the river except the regular Hudson's Bay Company boats.

—

Well, we started at 10:30. Passed two government policemen and took their coats and bags aboard. Les is very polite I assure you. No wonder everybody knows him.

At the Kitselas tunnels our things were stored in the watchman's cabin and we crossed on the railroad ties the big shanty ice to town [Kitselas]. A regular store and a hotel. Got mama's letter and Marj's. Mail, boots, rubber coats, tobacco, canned apricots, canned beefsteak and onions (help, we tried it). Lamp wicks and matches, repair material of all kinds for the steam shovels and engines and last but not least cat and kitten.

After an hour of stray talk and corncob pipes and all the kittens I cared for we started on. Leslie suggested going to the Engineers. They (two with two helpers and Chinese cook) are in the employ of the GTP to look after this work, to keep track of square yards of rock, gravel and clay taken out, inspect level of grade etc.

Mr. Patterson who owns the store came in. He also owns the hotel etc. "Staying for dinner Leslie? Well you're coming right up to the house of course." And off we go. Mrs. Patterson is not at all surprised and very gracious. Mrs. P's sister had a phonograph that played all afternoon and a brilliant red carpet while two cupids with bows and arrows vied for honors with two beautiful English prints.

—

On the way back to Hardscrabble, a chap named Anderson was coming up so he and Les pumped the speeder. We stopped at camp to deliver the mail and get some coffee and came home. We both had our hands full of parcels. The ground was wet and I was tired but with a good supper and cake we washed dishes, cleaned up and went to bed.

And today is another glorious day.
I have reformed and you will hear from me often,
Bernice

SPRING 1912

"The old shovel, our only hope, broke yesterday and was out of commission for hours. All work above here is stopped, they will have no food supplies and no coal can get by here…"

Grand Trunk Pacific Camp 19. Bernice and Leslie lived nearby at Camp 22, Mile 112, in a temporary railway camp called Hardscrabble. The camps were set up all along the line of construction and were not meant to be permanent. When the work was finished and the contract was completed the men picked up the supplies and equipment, moved up the line and built their next camp. *Prince Rupert City and Regional Archives and the Museum of Northern BC, WP997-107-14134*

A sure sign of spring along the lower Skeena River was a dog team going through the river ice. In the spring of 1912 both a mail team and a one-horse sleigh were the unfortunate harbingers of spring. Mail, men and dogs were saved but the unlucky horse was lost.

Early spring was an anxious time for the movement of freight—the ice began to break up but sternwheelers could not yet churn their way upriver. Hazelton, a pioneer Hudson's Bay Company post since 1880, located on the confluence of the Skeena and Bulkley rivers, was the last stop for the sternwheelers and functioned in 1912 as a merchant town and freight centre. In spring, before the boats could force their way upriver, mail delays were common and at Hazelton the merchants' shelves ran low. Rail and mail contractors turned to the experienced First Nations river men who stood in the large freight canoes and used long poles to pull themselves slowly upriver. Or the men strapped packs onto dogs and their own backs and under enormous weight walked the mail and store supplies over their well-travelled trails.

In April 1912 the work along the north side of the Skeena River was being completed and most camps and men were packed up, or, in the case of Leslie, finishing up the contract and in the process of cleaning up camp. The tracklayer and men waited for the bridge building gang to finish the 930-foot (283-metre) long, six-span bridge called Skeena Crossing 165 miles (266 kilometres) inland.

Work was underway farther up the Bulkley River from the recently established town of New Hazelton. Hundreds of men cleared and levelled the rail grade, built culverts and filled deep gaps. Duncan Ross had a huge camp of men who worked on clearing three long tunnels to skirt around Bulkley Canyon three miles (five kilometres) east of New Hazelton. Subcontractors' camps were established from New Hazelton southeast to Telkwa and from Telkwa east to Burns Lake so that blocks of track were worked on simultaneously, slowly pushing the railbed east. From the confluence of the Telkwa and Bulkley rivers John Bostrom had eight miles, then moving east Freeberg and Stone had ten miles, Hugh McLeod the next four miles, Smith the following seventeen miles, John Albi the next ten miles from Bulkley Summit westward, Duncan Ross ten miles from Bulkley Summit eastward, John McLeod five miles, A.L. McHugh ten miles, Dan Stewart ten miles, and D.A. Rankin fourteen miles along Burns Lake and eastward.

Camps needed stock replenished and the constant construction required new materials. Ordering supplies for the Hardscrabble Camp no doubt would have been stressful for Leslie Martin. Transporting heavy loads in early spring was near to impossible; the heavily travelled roads turned to mud. Wagons were often mired in massive mudholes and two or three teamsters usually travelled together to help each other out.

The spring thaw flooded streams and raised river levels dramatically. Construction inland from Hazelton, near the Bulkley River and over many tributary creeks, was set back as new fills washed out and streams suddenly appeared where no culverts had been placed. The newly completed line along the Skeena was tested and in some places failed.

Steam shovels were used to clear and level the rail grade. This one is working eastward toward the Skeena River, approaching Skeena Crossing. *Bulkley Valley Museum, P0381*

Track washouts were common and anything resembling scheduled train service was impossible. One man, on his way upriver from Prince Rupert to the end of steel just before Skeena Crossing, rode five different trains and walked a total of forty miles (sixty-four kilometres), taking over forty-eight hours to finally reach his home in Hazelton.

Repairing washouts and landslides was a headache for the contractors and a backache for the labourers. Steam shovels sank and overturned while trying to remove slides, and men were badly burned or injured in accidents as temporary tracks gave out. With the steam shovels proven to be useless and even dangerous, the labourers waded through cold mud to fix the rail grade and haul out the machinery with shovels, pry bars, buckets, ropes and block and tackle.

Hazelton's *Omenica Miner* reported that a large number of construction workers were loafing about town as a result of a wage reduction from $3 a day to $2.75 a day. A group of unsatisfied labourers under the banner of the Industrial Workers of the

World (IWW) walked off their jobs in protest of their poor camp conditions, their low hourly wage, long workday and lack of proper hospital facilities.

Although Bernice never wrote home about the strife with labourers, subcontractors such as D.A. Rankin and bookkeeper Leslie were affected. Both Foley, Welch and Stewart and the Grand Trunk Pacific were concerned that labour troubles would slow the pace of construction. Sir William Mackenzie said he would let the men strike until they were sick of it and denied claims of unsanitary camp conditions.

The IWW complained about the hospital deductions from their pay and pointed out the only medical facilities offered near the camps were rough shacks with an unfortunate medical student trying to help with what little medical supplies he had. As for the camp conditions, they claimed some were so poor "even a self respecting pig would refuse to die in it."

The labourers of the IWW tried to organize a walkout in May 1912 but

Three of the Kitselas tunnels blasted clear and levelled out. The newly laid steel track provided passenger and freight service up the line toward Skeena Crossing. *Prince Rupert City and Regional Archives and the Museum of Northern BC, RWPA 95787*

the contractors announced that on the first sign of trouble they would withdraw all the food supply from the camps. A walkout in such an isolated, sparsely populated region meant a walk of ten or fifteen miles (sixteen to twenty-four kilometres) to the nearest roadhouse that offered a tin plate of beans served on a stump for fifty cents.

The cries of some of the discontented labourers simmered down for the rest of the spring but many chose to leave. Railroad contractors were forced to look for labourers in the communities of New Hazelton, Aldermere and Telkwa, some stopping short of hauling farmers off their fields. Despite the tough working conditions and labour unrest a steady stream of new men arrived in Prince Rupert and rode the work trains to the first camp that handed them a shovel and a pair of boots.

With the right-of-way cleared in sections through the Bulkley Valley and the grade built in bits and pieces throughout, the GTP moved forward and established eight residencies between Aldermere in the Bulkley Valley and Burns Lake. At these residencies an engineer watched the work in his assigned area and reported back to Foley, Welch and Stewart on the progress of their subcontractors. Engineer Mr. Ehlrich was stationed at Residency 35.

First Nations

Prior to the construction of the Grand Trunk Pacific Railway the Tsimshian, the Nisga'a, the Gitxsan, the Wet'suwet'en and the Carrier Sekani had already experienced and were coping with the impacts of the Hudson's Bay Company, missionaries, surveyors and telegraph construction.

The First Nations people had complex social structures and governance and a specialized knowledge of plants, animals and their lands. They struggled to maintain their traditional knowledge and subsistence activities while the railway was built along their fishing sites, over their traplines and through their seasonal villages and sacred sites. Thousands of labourers moved along trails established by the First Nations and many hundreds of settlers moved in permanently to the newly established railway towns.

The First Nations people here today are a living testament to the tenacity and determination of their elders as many of their traditions are continued in their feast halls and on their traditional territories.

HARDSCRABBLE, BC
APRIL 6, 1912

My dear Daddy,

I have been thinking of you all day. How I would like to have you out here to see all the work just now. It is said that D.A. Rankin's Cut is known all along the line, south to Vancouver and east to Edmonton. You see it is the same piece of work that acted so badly last October and you ought to see it now.

Let me go back a little and tell you about the way the work is planned. The big company, Foley, Welch and Stewart, are building the rail grade. Their biggest contractor is D.A. Rankin. His piece of work in the first one hundred miles was not so bad but in his second hundred he had a long bad stretch and much trouble. In the first one hundred mile contract McDougall, the next biggest contractor, had a piece calling for a rock tunnel.

Well the whole thing came tumbling down, clay and gravel where the survey had said solid rock. They moved the tunnel to another place; of course this meant moving the grade and all. These men merely fill or cut, removing trees, streams, fields or mountains to do so and make the roadbed or trail. Then the RR Company lay the skeleton tracks. After McDougall's tunnel was all timbered and winter had set in the grade was finished up this far and made an elegant driving road. Then the RR laid their skeleton track to enable them to get supplies up to camp and that road bed is no good for man, beast nor RR train.

We have had some days of rain but the steam shovel had finished its work on each side of the cut and the enormous embankment, still rattling down rock and gravel, was left behind. The shovel moved to the lower end on the west side of the cut.

Its moving is most interesting. It stands on a section of track made of six rails which are moved almost right under it as it were. One day a landslide of a couple of tons pushed it off the track. When they want to move it they open the RR track to turn it and couple it onto the steam shovel track and out comes the shovel. The RR is then closed, the shovel moves down and then the RR opens again to let it come out in some other place.

They took the shovel apart to overhaul her and along the east bank four kyote holes were built and loaded with some hundred dollars' worth of powder. These are all shot together on a battery. Then the shovel digs and loads the little dump cars which the little engine pulls out.

Well, as I have said, we have had several days of rain. Part of the cut is gravel and part gray mud. As the rain kept on, the snow went off and this clay got wetter and wetter and came down in gobs and hunks and tons all into the cut. Little brooks broke through and it was one nice mess. But the rails were out of water and the shovel was moved.

Sunday evening a train came down from above and started into the cut. Four cars went off the track and there was devil to pay. To get them back up the men had to get covered in mud which by this time was waist-high. The track was covered and the rain was falling in torrents. They cut the train in two and after a twelve hour struggle cut the main end of the train out. Mr. Snell, foreman on the work, had four kyotes loaded and the water was ruining his powder and he was crazy.

Mrs. Snell and I walked over in the pouring rain. By much scrambling we got on the top of the bluff and walked to the edge of the cut. After a half-hour wait we came back home. Then, of course, the train was moved in ten minutes and the kyotes were fired. It was a lovely shot they said. The hole went bang, heaved and settled. They moved the shovel up and went to work bright and early. At about ten a slide occurred and buried the shovel as though she had been a wheelbarrow. A stream underground woke to life and caused some mischief. A hundred extra men are here in rubber boots and shovels doing their best to get the shovel out. No trains here for at least a week.

—

Les went over before breakfast and said all the brains of the GTPRR are here. Leslie did not come home at noon so I expect he had a busy day. Supplies of food or rubber boots, a stove for the extra shack for the extra men, or horseshoe nails for us to use as nut picks, he forgets nothing.

Les brought Dan Dempsey home to dinner, luckily I had a roast and cabbage salad. Dempsey is the supervisor of track-laying. He is one of the types of figures in this country. He went to Dawson overland from Ashcroft via the telegraph trail. He is one of the many who did not find gold. Started with 7 packhorses, traveled seven months and went to Dawson with all his worldly goods on his back.

Not a job for the faint of heart, the bridge-building gang helps Dan Dempsey and his track-laying crew across the Skeena River. With the completion of the Skeena Crossing Bridge the days of the sternwheeler were over; people and supplies now began to rely on the train.
Bulkley Valley Museum, P501

Today, Tony the Italian is putting tin over a shelf in the kitchen for me. I can understand what Helen Case meant when she said, "The most notable result of European civilization in India is the ever present standard oil tank." Here there are tin cans a foot square and two or more feet high and do duty in many capacities. I have two for waste water. Just inside the top is a wood handle. Down at Brown's camp in Newtown they use them as water pails. The men carry water two at a time with a neck yoke and ropes.

This weather is playing havoc with the cut. No progress can be made. The old shovel, our only hope, broke yesterday and was out of commission for hours. All work above here is stopped, they will have no food supplies and no coal can get by here. Les said D.A. Rankin wired from Spokane so details have gone his way.

In this piece of work they have taken out 307,000 cubic yards of earth gravel and mud. From the first of the work up to Feb 10th this work cost the RR, that is the old Rankin via Foley, Welch and Stewart, $300,000. Since then, to the end of March, another $10,000. The outfit—steam shovel, two engines, two trains, dumps cars, ties, etc. and running expenses—FWS furnish and so much rental. At present, during bad weather, expense to Rankin is $200 per day. This gives you some idea of the work.

The Pioneer Tracklayer

When the rumble of the wooden ties, the screech of the donkey engine and the clanging of steel rails was heard along the rail grade, residents of pioneer communities came out to watch the passing of the tracklayer. Photographs were taken all along the line of men, women and children watching Dan Dempsey and his crew of over one hundred men working in, on and around the strange-looking track-laying machine.

The tracklayer, called the Pioneer, did not do what its name implied. It did not lay the track. Instead, it carried all the steel, connective plates and ties needed for the track to be built. It saved labour by conveying the ties to the front and laying the steel on top of the ties.

The tracklayer was a series of linked cars. The first car held a steam donkey engine to power the track-laying machine. The first car also had a wooden frame for dragging and hoisting the sections of rail and a tall wooden structure from where the track boss

ABOVE: The Pioneer Tracklayer and the track-laying team near Hazelton, 1912. *Bulkley Valley Museum, P1622*

continued...

watched his men. On the upper plat-form two men lined up the rails and then laid them down. The locomotive engine was next, then a flatcar loaded with steel rails and connecting plates, followed by flatcars stacked high with wooden ties. On either side of the cars were wooden troughs with spiked roll-ers used for shunting ties to the front of the tracklayer. The conveyor troughs projected well ahead of the tracklayer.

The locomotive engine pushed the tracklayer to the end of steel. With the yelling of the track-laying boss and the screeching, clanging and pounding of the men and materials, construction would commence.

Men on the last car threw ties onto the conveyor, while those at the front laid ties as quickly as they came down the conveyor. Workers on the steel car connected plates to the long rails, which were caught by the men on the tracklayer, pulled over to the front and lowered onto the ties. The free end of the steel track was caught on the last connecting plate, bolts were slipped through and spikes were driven here and there linking the plates to the ties and holding the rail in place.

Work was carried out quickly and the newly laid rails often spread and sagged under the weight of the track-layer.

Another team of men followed the track-laying crew. They aligned and levelled the track by prying up ties and placing ballast under them. These men also spiked every rail.

Now I will close and send this to camp by Tony in hopes some good fellow will take it to the train.

Bushels of love,

Bernice

HARDSCRABBLE, BC
APRIL 11, 1912

My dear Mother,

The river is half open here before our door and it will soon be free of ice. As soon as possible the boats will be starting up. Leslie wants me to go to Prince Rupert as soon as possible and come back on the first boat. Regular passengers won't run, just the various freighters and not so many of them as last year. So I must catch my ride when I can. Then I will get all the little things which I have not here that I need.

After supper Leslie and I walked back over to the cut and through it. Dempsey has a track through after a week of fight with the mud. For a section about five rails long, the ties lie together like a float or raft and many of them were out of

Subcontractor D.A. Rankin and dog outside a camp building at Decker Lake. *Bulkley Valley Museum, P2868*

sight because the mud would run over them in a stream. We had to go carefully there for a misstep meant mud over my boots.

By the way, we at last got our mirror hung, tipped forward so I could see below my waist and oh, ye gods and little fishes, my lovely just washed sweater was a sight. Such spots of half-washedness. I asked Leslie why he had not told me how I looked and he said he thought I knew. Me for the naptha soap suds and no exertion at all—the loveliest white sweater you ever saw, from now on I swear by naptha for everything.

Someday I will get the camera films to a developer. The service is a bum. A box of green paper which came safely as far as Newtown just vanished into thin air. Les said probably some trainman ate it.

Bushels of love,

Bernice

Skeena River Sternwheelers

The *Union* was the first sternwheeler to attempt the Skeena. In 1864 she made it to a point just below the present day city of Terrace. Two years later the *Mumford* successfully navigated upriver to Kitsumkalum, delivering supplies for the construction teams working on the Collins Overland Telegraph. By 1891, the Hudson's Bay Company sternwheelers began making frequent runs up the Skeena River to Hazelton.

The Grand Trunk Pacific and Foley, Welch and Stewart began using sternwheelers on the Skeena River in 1908. They first supplied men and materials to the lower Skeena camps. As camps moved inland the sternwheelers made regular stops at Kitselas, Skeena Crossing and Hazelton. Hazelton was generally agreed to be the end of navigable waters and a natural staging point for the men and materials.

The Skeena River sternwheelers were busy. In *Where the Rivers Meet* J. Glen Senior writes, "Lumberjacks, teamsters, miners and muckers rubbed shoulders with contractors, resident engineers and bankers from the small

Grand Trunk Pacific Railway President Charles Hays heavily promoted the northern railway. He was confident the new port city of Prince Rupert would be successful. From aboard the *Port Simpson* GTP in August of 1910, President Hays tours the beginning of construction on the lower Skeena. *Bulkley Valley Museum, P0384*

mushroom towns which were springing up along the right-of-way adjacent to the Skeena. Teams of horses for freighters, miscellaneous railroad equipment, construction camp supplies, sacks of oats and baled hay. The deck was reserved for heavy equipment, cordwood and kerosene drums."

The Grand Trunk Pacific and Foley, Welch and Stewart had five sternwheelers; they were named the *Skeena*, the *Operator*, the *Conveyor*, the *Distributor* and the *Omenica*.

NEWTOWN
APRIL 15, 1912

Dear Mother,

In the afternoon D.A. Rankin came in from Rupert. He had to come in to look over the work and to see for himself that the cut was alright at Hardscrabble.

Les and he went above to Mile 156 where he has a camp at work so I had to come away. Chris Anderson and Chris the blacksmith and I came in the speeder Wednesday. Les will come down to take me home.

Al Brown keeps talking to me. This letter is as foolish as Al's conversation but I want to tell you I love you all dearly.

The ice is going out in the river but not yet fit for the ferry at Kitselas so we won't get our mail for a week.

Give my love to the dear ones.

Bernice

HARDSCRABBLE
SUNDAY, APRIL 21, 1912

My dearest Mother,

We have such a gorgeous day. The ice is gone and the river has raised five inches in 24 hours.

Now I have to go tomorrow night to Newtown and stay at Browns' overnight so I can take the Tuesday am train to get me into Rupert in time to do some shopping and take the Port Simpson sternwheeler back up the river.

Mrs. Parker and young Jimmie are coming back from Prince Rupert with me. The trip back upriver will take several days, depending on how long the boat happens to stick on the sand bars and how well it holds its power against the current. I am so glad to have the trip. The evenings are frosty but the days gorgeous.

Today I dried my hair in a twinkling out of doors. We planted a bed of radishes, lettuce, onions and parsley. We buy Cowichan guaranteed eggs at 40 cents a dozen when we buy a case at Hazelton. Plain eggs are just 33 cents per dozen.

Charles Melville Hays
May 16, 1856–April 15, 1912

Described as the "moving spirit behind the Grand Trunk Pacific Railway," Charles Melville Hays died on April 15, 1912, on the RMS *Titanic*. Newspapers speculated Hays would have been one of the men who helped place women and children in the lifeboats and stayed to go down with the ship. The *Omenica Herald* mourned the passing of Mr. Hays but announced that Mrs. Hays and daughter Marguerite were saved.

Charles Melville Hays was the Grand Trunk Pacific's biggest political supporter; his predictions of heavy rail traffic, booming towns and destination cities were almost foolishly optimistic.

Upon hearing of the death of Mr. Hays and realizing the significance of the loss, the Grand Trunk Pacific issued orders that all stations and stops with a flag were to lower it to half-mast.

The first canoe to carry freight was due past here today but we missed it if it did go by.

Leslie, a man named William Tuck and D.A. Rankin have a contract in at Burns Lake. This is direct from the RR and not through Foley, Welch and Stewart. Leslie is so happy to be on the ground floor at last. Look on the GTPRR folder map and find Aldermere. By the first of the year the field will be that far but now there is a 180 mile freight haul from some small town in to Decker Lake, just below and east of South Bulkley. The warehouse will be there and we will live in a cabin near it. Decker Lake is 8 miles long and portages to Burns Lake some 18 miles long. Thru there the freight will go by boat.

Every bit of lumber will be hand hewn so you see we will be very simply housed. Leslie goes in sometime in June to get things started and I will go down below for a while. Seattle or Vancouver? If you will join me for a month just watch me come.

Is not this a newsy letter?

Give my love to all and make the shameful confession for me that I have not written one note.

Love to my dear family,

Bernice

HARDSCRABBLE, BC
MAY 17, 1912

My dear Ruth,

Leslie has gone to the interior and left me with my house, the kittens and the kindness of my neighbors. It is not so bad. Mrs. Ross, a very dear woman who has been living in Newtown, is coming up on the boat for a visit. She can't come today for the river is so high the boats can't get through the canyon just now. It rose three feet in 30 hours but has gone down ten inches in the last 12 hours. If she does not come for three days I can make quite a hole in my correspondence.

In Prince Rupert last week the yards were full of skunk cabbages where the town had not been graded but here the first tiny green leaves are only just now coming.

This letter is going to camp to try to get to Newtown for Sunday's train.

Love,

Bernice

SUMMER 1912

"Most of the people here are Canadian; they cook their tea, say bath instead of bathe and prayers are offered for the King, Queen, Prince of Wales and so on."

JULY 7TH 1912 PHOTO W.W.W.
G.T.P PASSENGER TRAIN LEAVING SKEENA CROSSING

A GTP passenger train leaving Skeena Crossing travelling east to South Hazelton, July 1912. *Bulkley Valley Museum, P1920*

Railroaders on the GTP moved camp often. They followed the clearing of the land, the levelling of the grade and the laying of the track inland. Wives and children, rooming houses, merchants, restaurants, laundries, livery stables and illegal liquor establishments referred to as "blind pigs" followed the movement of the contracts inland.

Summer meant an increase in pace for construction. The drier roads allowed easier movement of freight and the long northern day length meant labour proceeded late into evening hours before the night shift lit the lanterns. Foley, Welch and Stewart estimated in July 1912 that 2,772 men were at work between Skeena Crossing and Burns Lake.

Officials took advantage of the favourable travelling conditions and inspected the rail grade. In early June, Patrick Welch of Foley, Welch and Stewart took a steamer up from Vancouver to Prince Rupert and looked over the work of his subcontractors. On the steamer with Welch were a large number of workhorses and over two hundred labourers recruited for work along the line between New Hazelton and Burns Lake.

The completion of the Skeena Crossing Bridge was a big occasion. Here the first Grand Trunk Pacific passenger train stops to allow the travellers a glimpse of the massive bridge at the historic first crossing in July 1912. *Bulkley Valley Museum, P1923*

The railway must have met official standards by this time because in July the premier of British Columbia, Sir Richard McBride, and Attorney General W.J. Bowser, travelled inland on a special train to Hazelton and saw for themselves the progress of construction. Accompanying the premier and Attorney General on the special train was W.C.C. Mehan, general superintendent of the western division of the Grand Trunk Pacific and G.A. McNichol, district superintendent. Upon arrival in Hazelton, the premier spoke glowingly of the development of the district, the mineral potential, the agricultural success and the obvious prosperity of the region.

In late July, the chief engineer of the Grand Trunk Pacific, B.B. Kelliher, and Department of Railways engineer, Collingwood Schreiber, travelled together on a horse-drawn stage to inspect the grade between Hazelton and Aldermere.

In the early summer months of 1912, the Grand Trunk Pacific exerted control on the riverboats and gained priority shipping for railway materials and camp supplies.

Skeena Crossing Bridge

Up the river 160 miles (258 kilometres) from Prince Rupert is Skeena Crossing, a bridge over the Skeena River that took hundreds of men years to complete. The bridge is a stunning 945 feet (288 metres) long and 164 feet (50 metres) high.

Due to the massive construction efforts at Skeena Crossing a little town of temporary workers' shacks sprung up in 1911 with 140 men living there under the watchful eye of Captain McLeod. By 1912, the number of men had doubled and work was in earnest.

Foley, Welch and Stewart established a freight depot nearby to unload supplies from the Skeena sternwheelers. And unload supplies they did; approximately thirty-one sternwheeler-loads of cement were required for the piers of Skeena Crossing, one million feet (three hundred thousand metres) of lumber and forty tons of iron were used for the caissons that were sunk in the river within which the excavation for the foundations were made.

The Skeena Crossing Bridge was completed in July 1912. *Bulkley Valley Museum, P1922*

continued...

Winter of 1912 saw progress on the caissons; the first of these watertight boxes was completed in March. The piers were begun and the second caisson was sunk and sealed in April. When work on the piers was nearing completion in April 1912, the steelwork started.

In the summer of 1912, as work on Skeena Crossing neared completion, the *Inlander* sternwheeler took one hundred Hazelton locals on an excursion to the bridge. The *Inlander's* captain, J.H. Bonser, who first captained sternwheelers on the Skeena for the Hudson's Bay Company twenty years earlier, realized that the completion of Skeena Crossing meant the end of riverboats on the Skeena River.

The tracklayer travelled across the Skeena Crossing in July 1912 and by the end of the summer passenger trains began crossing on their way to end of steel near New Hazelton.

The embargo on Hazelton merchants was such that a June issue of the *Omenica Miner* was printed on brown wrapping paper because the order for white paper sat unshipped at the Prince Rupert warehouses. The Hazelton merchants banded together and lobbied the Grand Trunk Pacific and Foley, Welch and Stewart for equal treatment. Soon goods flowed both along the rail tracks and on the Skeena River.

Farmers who ordered farm implements saw them arrive in time for harvest. In August there were piles of agricultural equipment at the Hudson's Bay Company warehouse at Hazelton ready for shipping to the Bulkley Valley. Farmers reported expanded livestock operations and record harvests. The pioneer ranches that were established long before the rail construction started in Prince Rupert enjoyed hard-earned success as men and camps demanded fresh farm produce and hundreds of workhorses required feed. Farmers planted hundreds more root crops and enjoyed the fact that their hay was selling for an amazing $60 a ton.

Mineral exploration in the mountains surrounding Hazelton, Aldermere and Telkwa expanded. Miners counted on the railway to ease their isolation and shorten their distance to markets; they imported the needed equipment and stockpiled ore samples for future export. Summer was a boom time for the mines. In August 1912,

Charlie Barrett

Charles "Charlie" Barrett came to northern British Columbia leading a three-hundred animal pack train for the construction of the Dominion Telegraph Line. When the project ended in 1902, Barrett, in partnership with J.K. Sealy and Ed Charleson, started a 320-acre ranch six miles (about ten kilometres) north of Houston on the east side of the Bulkley River near the junction with the Morice River and named it the Diamond D Ranch. Also called the Home Ranch, the Diamond D expanded to 3,120 acres by 1908.

The Diamond D Ranch was a stunning success. In the summer of 1908, five hundred tons of hay were cut, worth about $20,000 by 1908 prices. Charlie Barrett employed fifteen men, grew hull-less barley, oats, potatoes and fall-sown wheat, and raised cattle, hogs and horses.

J.K. Sealy withdrew from the partnership and started his own very successful ranch near the Moricetown-to-Aldermere wagon road in the Bulkley Valley. In 1910 Charleson also left the partnership and Charles Barrett became the sole owner of all the holdings. The area where Barrett farmed became

Haying on Charlie Barrett's Diamond D Ranch, summer 1912. *Bulkley Valley Museum, P0913*

known as South Bulkley.

The Home Ranch was an enormous undertaking consisting of a large ranch house with nine bedrooms, a boarding house, a bunkhouse, hay sheds, a blacksmith shop, three stables, five mowers, five wagons, a binder and a threshing machine. By the time the construction of the Grand Trunk Pacific reached Barrett's ranch in 1912 it was one of the best-developed agricultural properties in the area.

Charlie met Helen, sister-in-law of Telkwa's Doctor Wallace, and the two were married and settled at Diamond D Ranch. Charlie Barrett lived the rest of his days at the ranch. He died in 1946. Barrett Lake west of Houston was named for Charlie, and Helen Lake, also west of Houston, was named for his wife.

mining recorder Mr. Kirby issued 71 miners' licences, recorded 116 claims, 26 agreements and transfers and issued 158 certificates of work.

In the summer of 1912, the bridge building gang moved on to Seeley Gulch, twelve miles (nineteen kilometres) inland from Skeena Crossing. Trains were allowed to cross the newly laid track on the Skeena Crossing Bridge and progressed slowly up the freshly ballasted track to the edge of Seeley Gulch. The end of steel waited for the concrete piers over Seeley Gulch to be completed. Freight and passengers were unloaded at the end of the tracks and transported at their own expense into the next community, now South Hazelton. South Hazelton was just three miles (about five kilometres) west of New Hazelton and both towns were in a fierce competition for the station and railway development.

But it was not all progress along the line. The IWW rallied together again and in July 1912, they completely shut down work between New Hazelton and Burns Lake. Labourers drew their pay and left the area. Some were tempted to the prairies for harvest time there. Others headed to Prince Rupert and never returned. The Foley, Welch and Stewart teamsters continued to haul freight and somehow work continued despite the number of workers falling from 2,772 in July to 1,400 in August.

The IWW rendezvoused at Prince Rupert and met men who disembarked from coastal steamers hoping to find work on the GTP. Fifty potential labourers were stopped and only three continued upriver to find jobs east of New Hazelton. A plan was launched to starve the strikers out and an angry Martin Welch stated that "…the only place to get food supplies is the construction camp and you don't suppose the contractors will let a lot of agitators loaf there." The strikers responded that the food was of poor quality and not properly cooked. Contractors ignored their complaints and brought in men from the coast. Foley, Welch and Stewart placed ads in newspapers to recruit labourers throughout southern BC and the United States.

The IWW made no progress on their demands for better pay, shorter days and improved camp conditions. Some returned to work and the *Omenica Herald* reported in August 1912 that the IWW agitators had moved on to the Rockies to stir up unrest on the GTP construction there.

The camp and railway community on the shores of Decker Lake. *Bulkley Valley Museum P538*

HARDSCRABBLE, JUNE 1912
[LETTER FROM LESLIE FRANK MARTIN TO BERNICE'S FATHER]

My Dear Mr. Medbury:

As we are all through in this camp and are cleaning up the territory going on to the next job I thought I would let you know something of my plans for your daughter Bernice and myself.

Bernice said she has written you in regard to the fact that I was to have an interest in the new work at Burns Lake, 150 miles inland from Hazelton.

I made a trip there recently. I went from here to Skeena Crossing, where they are putting a large bridge across the Skeena River, by train. From Skeena Crossing I took the boat to Hazelton. Foley, Welch and Stewart have their warehouse at Sealey, which is three miles this side of Hazelton on the river. From Sealey I took Rankin's driving team to Aldermere, which is about 50 miles from Hazelton. There are two towns lying close together, Aldermere and Telkwa. Aldermere is on the hill on the main wagon road and Telkwa is down near the Bulkley River.

Aldermere is the smaller of the two but is on a direct line of travel through the Bulkley Valley. I took the team as far as Barrett's ranch 25 miles from Aldermere.

Barrett has been in this country for quite a few years. He got his start by pack-

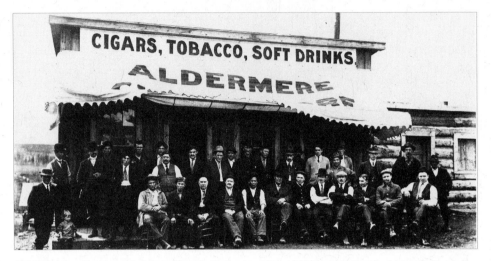

Aldermere merchants and residents. Joseph Coyle, the editor of Aldermere's *Interior News*, is standing in the back row on the right and his young daughter Ellen Coyle is sitting on a stump. *Bulkley Valley Museum, P1247*

ing government supplies over the trail between Ashcroft, on the CPR main line, and Hazelton and also further north towards the Yukon on the telegraph line. His ranch is the best in this country and shows lots of hard work getting it in shape.

From there I took a saddle horse to Burns Lake which is a three day trip. I had to arrange each day to make a stopping place at night where there was feed for my horses. The wagon road is built within 50 miles of camp so I could not bring the team. That left me 75 miles to make with a saddle horse. About 25 miles of wagon road and 50 over trail.

They have started, since I came back, to build the wagon road on to Decker Lake, about 18 miles from the camp we have built. Decker Lake is about 11 miles long and is connected with Burns Lake by a small stream.

When the wagon road is finished we will break to the head of Decker Lake where a warehouse will be built and from there we will freight by gas boat to the various camps.

There is about 13 miles of work let to D.A. Rankin Company, which they in turn

Aldermere and Telkwa

Aldermere was located on a ridge near Tyhee Lake, above present-day Telkwa. Aldermere was first staked in 1904 by North Coast Land Company agent, John Dorsey, and became a convenient stop along the wagon road. The community had a hotel, newspaper, jail, rooming house, blacksmith, laundry, horse stables and enough permanent residents to host some lively community parties.

Telkwa, just down the hill from Aldermere near the confluence of the Telkwa and Bulkley rivers, was surveyed in 1907. It soon had a church, merchants and permanent residents.

The construction of the railway caused a temporary boom in Aldermere due to the freighters moving equipment inland through Aldermere heading for Bulkley Summit and Rose, Decker and Burns lakes. But when the GTP established a depot near Telkwa the wagon road was made all but obsolete. Aldermere declined as most of the merchants moved down the hill to be closer to the station stop village of Telkwa. Once the creation of the new town of Smithers was announced in 1913 it was Telkwa that hoped to survive by retaining businesses and providing retail competition. A major fire destroyed Telkwa's stores in 1914 and most merchants chose to rebuild in Smithers. Although not a major retail centre, Telkwa is still a thriving community today.

The freight transfer station at Telkwa. When the Grand Trunk Pacific began shipping and receiving goods on their trains the use of the wagon road greatly decreased and the community of Aldermere declined. *Bulkley Valley Museum, P0040.*

The pioneer settlement of Telkwa. *Bulkley Valley Museum, P0694*

will sublet to Harry Rankin, William Tuck and myself. D.A. Rankin will retain a quarter interest for himself leaving us each a quarter. This is sublet to us at about 10 cents a yard less than D.A. Rankin gets. They are to give us the use of what outfit has been in use at Mile 156 and Hardscrabble where they have contracts. Also they guarantee us wages at the rate of $125 per month and board.

Tuck told me that he had it figured that we could make about $8,000 apiece by subletting it in turn to station men to take one or two cuts or small dots off it. Of course this is something one cannot always figure on. It is an entering wedge for better work where money can be made. Also I will have a little ready money to invest in Fort George and Prince Rupert real estate which ought to be good when this railroad is finished.

In this work at Burns Lake, Tuck will have the outside work and I the inside work. Harry Rankin will look after the camp. That is the way it is planned at present.

I stopped to explain about the work as it came to mind. I spent two days at Burns Lake then started for home. Coming from Aldermere I made 36 miles in one afternoon with the driving team over bad roads. They are certainly a fine team. Fifty miles a day is nothing for them.

We expect the track to be laid to Aldermere this coming winter which will give us a shorter haul. While it [the general cost of living] is higher there, prices on goods are lower than here, as Foley, Welch and Stewart furnishes them to us on a 10% basis and they get a free haul from Prince Rupert.

Bernice always tells me she is quite content here and I think she will like it in there. The country is open and there are plenty of places to go with a saddle horse and canoe. She looks the picture of health. We intend to go to Rupert to celebrate Dominion Day July 1st and perhaps the fourth.

With best regards to yourself and the rest of your family.

I am yours,

Leslie Frank Martin

HAZELTON, BC
JULY 17, 1912

My dear Vivian,

We left our happy home at Hardscrabble for a three-day trip which has been lengthened into more than two weeks.

Leslie has gone into the interior to inspect new work, start camp building and our new home.

In this country everything moves or stands at the call of the RR. Just now wonderful progress is being made but in ten days the rails and with them the construction trains will stop at Seeley Gulch where a big bridge has to be erected.

The road lies in the river valley and to watch the work of cut and fill, bridge and tunnel has been so fascinating that I have been out of doors most every minute of daytime since I have been in BC.

Up here, 200 miles inland, the costs are almost prohibitive—fifty-one cents for a pineapple, eggs from the henhouse $1 dozen. At Burns Lake we hope to have chickens as I have not had any chicken but the tinned variety for six months. In Hazelton all the laundries offer, "Bath—50 cents."

Most of the people here are Canadian; they cook their tea, say bath instead of bathe and prayers are offered for the king, queen, Prince of Wales and so on. It seems so queer to such an American as I.

Best wishes to your mother and father.

Lovingly yours,

Bernice Medbury Martin

Patrick Burns
(1856–1937)

Patrick Burns, *Glenbow Museum NA-1149-1*

continued...

Pat Burns was a clever entrepreneur who realized that there was a need for fresh beef in the railway construction camps and pioneer towns. He aggressively filled that need by buying cattle in large numbers and driving the animals long distances, over rugged terrain, to the sporadic towns and railway camps in northern British Columbia. Pat Burns catered to his clients; he even had Bobby Grant distribute free Christmas turkeys to camp men and pioneer families along the Skeena in 1908.

Pat Burns's business was always in the news and that was just the way he wanted it. The progress of the P.C. Burns cattle drives were tracked, with the latest updates passed along telegraph lines and reported in the early newspapers. When a Burns and Company cattle drive came to town they would sell the cattle "on the hoof" and proceed to the next community. Railroad camps often had a pen built and waiting for the Burns cattle.

The railway construction created a boom in the population and Burns successfully created a thriving meat business. Upon the completion of the Grand Trunk Pacific in 1914 he was noted as one of the most successful entrepreneurs in all of Canada.

The philanthropy of Pat Burns positively impacted communities throughout British Columbia and Alberta. As a result of his civic-mindedness there are parks, neighbourhoods, land, streets and schools named for him. Among these are Burns Bog in Delta, British Columbia, and Mount Burns in Alberta.

Willing to Pay

Hazelton, B.C.
McRae Bros.

The settlements in northern BC were far apart and prices rose exponentially the farther one travelled. Rail supplies, workhorses, farm implements and crates of food were brought to Prince Rupert by coastal steamer and went up the Skeena River along the newly completed line or on sternwheelers. From the end of steel or the riverboat landings the goods and supplies travelled over the rough rail grade to points beyond along the roughed-out trails and early roads by horseback, dog team, wagon and with the early solid-rubber wheeled vehicles. Coming from the opposite direction were long lines of heavily loaded pack horses shipping goods overland from the Lower Mainland up to Quesnel and along the telegraph trail to northwestern British Columbia.

Prices fluctuated wildly according to just how much a person was willing to pay. When the Foley, Welch and Stewart contractors needed hay for their horses they were willing to pay top

The pioneer community of Hazelton. *Bulkley Valley Museum, P1930*

continued...

price to get it, any of it. In the summer of 1912 hay sold for upwards of $60 a ton—this was likely the only time the farmers in northern BC really reaped their due rewards!

Agricultural land was sold at $500 for an eighty-acre farm. Investors were willing to pay for land in the rising cities. The 1912 sale of provincial government lots in Prince Rupert saw prices reach phenomenal numbers with one double-corner lot selling for $58,000.

Transportation was also expensive. Covering only a short distance, the Aldermere to Chicken Lake (present-day Lake Kathlyn) Mail Stage charged $3 for a one-way passenger ticket. The early automobile stages charged $15 for a one-way bumpy ride from New Hazelton to Aldermere and the cheapest coastal steamer fare out of Prince Rupert was $11 for "deck passage."

When road conditions were poor the freighters increased their price per pound. People isolated in the Interior paid what the freighters charged for their crates of supplies. Men's suits sold for $30, a Stetson hat for $7.50 and a saddle cost $70. One yard of lace was $3.50 and eggs sold for 75 cents a dozen. Water was delivered to homes for 75 cents a barrel. Five Roses household flour was $3 a sack, a box of apples was advertised at $3.50 and rubber boots cost $4 a pair. One small bottle of whiskey was sold by the illegal liquor establishments for $6.

Advertised prices for basic goods steadily increased during the Grand Trunk Pacific construction days but one rate remained steady. The Grand Trunk Pacific labourers were paid just $2.75 a day by Foley, Welch and Stewart.

FALL 1912

"Next time I shall carry out
my threat to make a tent out of a
sheet and stick. You see I have to wait
here. First, till the cabin should be
roofed and, now, for a chance
to ride out."

A mud street through the temporary tent town that was located between Decker Lake and Burns Lake. *Bulkley Valley Museum, P2853*

Fall was harvest time throughout the North; a time when the abundance of wild-life was apparent. A man could dip a bucket in the Skeena River for water and come up with his dinner too—a four-pound (about two kilograms) rainbow trout in his pail. A ninety-five-pound (forty-three kilogram) spring salmon was caught near Hazelton; in 1912 this was the largest salmon on record. A five-point buck was shot near Hazelton. Grouse season opened up and as a result birds were scarce around the pioneer towns. Hudson's Bay Company wagons pulled by strong four-horse teams hauled 3,500 pounds (1,600 kilograms) of furs out of Hazelton.

Farmers harvested crops and were so proud of their achievements that they formed the Bulkley Valley Agricultural Association. This association organized the first annual exhibition of Northern Interior products held in Telkwa, setting the foundation for an annual fall fair that continues to this day. The fair showed a profusion of farm products and livestock as well as a large display of ore.

The optimism of the prospectors and miners in the North was backed up by several sensational strikes. A claim on Fiddler Creek created a little stampede of speculators. The Hazelton district showed silver lead ores that carried very high gold content. A chance bushfire revealed an outcropping of a vein on which a number of claims were instantly staked. The goldfields surrounding Hazelton and north of Hazelton were, in 1912, thought to be some of the richest in the world.

Winter came early to the mines at higher elevations. There was a scarcity of feed for horses in the mountains. All but the hardiest of miners left their mountain claims for one of the pioneer towns or they chose to take the steamers "down below" to Vancouver, Victoria and Seattle. With the Skeena Crossing Bridge completed, the large team of labourers employed on the Foley, Welch and Stewart bridge building gang had moved on to the next large obstacle—a 194-foot (59-metre) deep gorge called Seeley Gulch. There were many delays here and it took the entire fall for the 902-foot (275-metre) long steel bridge structure to be completed, with over one week dedicated to riveting alone. Once the bridge building men completed the crossing, the eager track-laying crew moved in and soon a track was laid to the prospective townsite of South Hazelton. In November the Grand Trunk Pacific granted permission for trains to carry freight and passengers over Seeley Gulch to South Hazelton.

After being stuck high and dry on the river rocks for a number of weeks, the *Inlander* took advantage of the higher water levels in mid-September, tooted her last salute to Hazelton and churned downriver to Prince Rupert. With passengers and freight being carried over Skeena Crossing and on to South Hazelton by rail, the days of the sternwheeler on the Skeena River were over. The tooting of the sternwheeler was no more and the whistle of the Grand Trunk Pacific locomotive became a familiar sound in the Interior.

In the fall of 1912 Leslie Martin was at Decker Lake where he helped keep track of supplies and set up large camps for D.A. Rankin. Leslie was not only under pressure to prepare Rankin's camp but he also had to build a log house. While the cabin was being built Bernice waited at Ehlrich's camp near Bulkley Summit, called Residency 35. Here Bernice met Mrs. Ehlrich, wife of the residency engineer in charge of overseeing the contracts in the area. Bernice stayed as a guest in Mrs. Sprauge's large tent while Danley D. Sprauge worked nearby as a bridge engineer. Bernice was impatient at the inconsistent pace of the railway construction and her inability to travel inland to her new home at Decker Lake.

SEPTEMBER 8, 1912
GTP RESIDENCY #35, BULKLEY VALLEY

Dearest Daddy,

Mrs. Sprauge, with whom I am tenting while Leslie builds the proverbial pumpkin shell, is a perfectly charming woman. Up here everyone takes things as they come. Here I have been for ten days and no one thinks it strange nor seems surprised when a message comes from Leslie to wait a few more days.

Here we get up and breakfast at about 7. Then I sew and read and talk and sew and read and talk and at 12 eat. Then I sew and read and sew and read and at 6 eat. Then I sew and read and talk and at 9 sleep. I have embroidered a pillow as far as my thread goes, have made little handkerchiefs as I have linen for and have read everything good, bad or indifferent at hand.

It's hard to write as there are so many interruptions.

This morning Mrs. Sprauge and I went out to a natural meadow just beyond here so I could get some snapshots of the pack train and 24 horses and the three packers. The GTP pack train packing supplies in for the engineer's camp above here. I got two of the men strapping the yokes and one of the train in motion.

This afternoon steers came through here on the government road—400 of them. That is the way the Pat Burns Company is bringing all beef into the country. It is a very welcome change from the old method of shipping in refrigerating boats up from lower BC to Prince Rupert then up to anywhere from 56 to 256 miles by boat and train with no attempt at sanitation.

All along the road at every eating house or camp there is a stockade or pen with a great windmill sort of structure for slaughtering. The pen here is 16 feet high and the steers jumped it and for ten days the cowboys and butchers wandered about hunting them. All that time we have had ham and ham and ham.

Grand Trunk Pacific Camp 35. Mrs. Sprauge's home near Bulkley Summit—Mrs. Sprauge with trout, Mrs. Ehlrich with grouse. *Bulkley Valley Museum, P0529*

Every day is a fresh disappointment. Next time I shall carry out my threat to make a tent out of a sheet and stick. You see I have to wait here. First, till the cabin should be roofed and, now, for a chance to ride out. I could borrow a saddle horse but should have to ride 20 miles in one day and when I don't know how anyway that could be pretty stiff. And besides some man from the contractors camp will have to go with me making a two day trip for him. That is the way it is up here, like checker men we wait for someone to move us. But I have found a new friend, Mrs. Sprauge.

I feel as though Daddy will think I am complaining, I certainly did not mean it that way it is just the conditions of my country life.

The GTPRR mail boy is in and it is almost lunchtime so I must stop.

Mrs. Sprauge has a note from her husband. He had news from Prince Rupert about the sale of lots by the government. One corner lot sold for $58,000.

Les says he is catching lots of trout. We have had grouse twice. Some are called spruce grouse and taste of the spruce they have eaten.

Bernice

Real Estate Optimism

The Grand Trunk Pacific Railway construction caused wild speculation on the pace and depth of growth for towns in the Northwest. Prince Rupert and Fort George espoused the most guarantee for investments; Prince Rupert as the GTP rail terminus and transportation port, Fort George as the hub city to British Columbia's north, east, south and west.

The early settlers of Smithers, operating businesses and banks out of temporary buildings.
Bulkley Valley Museum, P2599

Other communities fought for investors, merchants and settlers. Each seemed to have equal claim to their likely successful future. Towns supported by large railway stations, sidings or roundhouse were thought likely to succeed. Joseph Coyle, of the *Interior News* in Aldermere, compared the towns' competition to a trickster's game of hiding a pea under shifting walnut shells: "watch the little townsite pea, watch the little townsite pea, now you see it, now you don't, railway wins and farmer loses."

New Hazelton was advertised as "the payroll town, the town with a future, the new home of millionaires." Early Smithers residents wore lapel pins that stated, "5,000 population by 1914." The "three best towns on the GTP main line" were advertised on a map with large stars over Prince Rupert, Hubert and Fort George. Telkwa was "sure to become one of the richest agricultural and mining districts in the world." Telkwa's development would be "marvellously rapid." The envisioned "Decker City" at Decker Lake was to boast a beautiful lakeside park that was sure to attract a large number of settlers. Other ads placed in newspapers boasted: "we can positively state Fort Fraser will be the largest city between Edmonton and Prince Rupert." Fort Fraser was the "coming city" offering "the best opportunity in Canada for large profits."

HOME SWEET HOME, DECKER LAKE, BC
SATURDAY MORNING, SEPTEMBER 28, 1912

My Dearest Mother,

Back I must go into medieval history about two weeks. You remember I kept writing about the man who was coming to pick me up at Ehlrich's? Well, when he did not arrive on the last succession of settled dates, I was sick with worry and waiting. So I went from the engineer's down half mile to the contractor's camp, Duncan Ross's big camp, where there is a telephone and called Les up and said, "Well young man!" He said, "I know it but what am I to do. No driving horses here and no one to leave here if there were horses." B: "This has gone beyond the point of a joke," (very sternly). L: "Well, if you feel it necessary I will see if I can't get someone to go for you." B: "Just do that then."

After supper Mr. Sherwood, the clerk at Ross's camp came up and said Mr. McLeod would be up for Mrs. Martin at about noon. I'd packed so many times with no avail that I would not start again. But he DID come and we started at about ten o'clock the next morning. Captain McLeod—once in the English navy—is as large as a peanut and looks much like one, with his sunburned face, khaki clothes and little cap. He drives a big red horse hitched to a buckboard and they hit squarely every other stump in the twelve miles at a dead run. The road is only seven weeks old. But the drive was beautiful, groves of yellow leaved poplars, soft springy dirt underfoot and yellow sunshine everywhere.

Once in awhile in an open we could see off for miles, over low rolling country— an occasional ranch, here and there we cross the old telegraph trail or a little stream. Up a long hill and out on top, there below us was a lovely lake.

Another town and we were at McLeod's camp, a row of long buildings as usual. We stopped for coffee. Now at 4:30 in the afternoon. Two things distinguish that camp—flies so thick you could not tell currant cakes and sugar cookies apart and heavy smoke from forest fires about 300 feet away. Frank Bowness had come up on saddle horse to meet me there and drive the rest of the way out. Up over a hill and the drop so sharp the horse sat down and slid.

Stopped at a roadhouse—a cooking and eating place with a sleeping tent. The owner "Dad" wrote to the cache for Worcester sauce and ketchup by the gallon. A new hand filled the order as received. A few days later just the same order came in and was filled just the same. Next came a letter—"When I order ketchup, I don't want ketchup, I want Scotch whiskey. When I order Worcester sauce, I don't want Worcester sauce, I want Rye Whiskey and don't you forget it." Thus the story goes.

One place is a big open flat and is being surveyed for Decker City. It is about three miles away from the lake.

Here is Les, the teams are being hitched for the switch so I will send the letter with them.

My best of love,

Bernice

DECKER LAKE, BC
OCTOBER 9, 1912

My dearest Daddy,
I think I should tell you of my arrival here.

Les and I struck the pine flats. The so-called lodge pole pines only grow two or four feet apart straight up from a six inch bottom at least 30 feet high to a tiny tip. Our roof in the cabin is made of them, in the whole 80 or more on a side and some 12 feet long to gable. I fail to see one inch of variation in size and no taper.

The road ambles on through pines on almost perfectly flat ground. If some fool had not forgotten to put out his campfire it would have been wonderful. As it was, it is rather pitiful to see all the bark and needles halfway up all blackened. Next year they will be peeled for someone's roof.

Well, to travel on. A tinkle of bells ahead of us and before long we overtook a four cayuse Indian outfit. Donald Boo of the famous family of Boo, the original inhabitants. Boo, by someone dubbed Sir Donald Boo, his wife Lady Lucy Boo, the daughter about 16 and a little Boo.

Then we crossed the right of way. As far as the eye could see a broad path had been cut through the trees as straight as a bird can fly. The log buildings showed up in the last of the sunset. First Doc Shaw's Roadhouse, some men loafing about and one making a bedstead out of poles, next a couple of tents at Stewart's Cache, and then a little log building nestled against a great log building the D.A. Rankin and Company office and warehouse. Next a log barn half roofed with canvas and straight ahead a good sized log building that was the palace Martin. And oh, woe is me, of charred logs. The windows and doors were in place. The roof walls and floor made a big dark interior. The dishes, pans, lamps etc. on a table in the kitchen and boxes and boxes and shavings, shavings, shavings. Home!

Some time since we exchanged letters. Living is so high—every move costs so much. One trip out to Hardscrabble cost Leslie $115 besides his railroad pass, his own team and his accommodation for the roadhouses. When he brought me out all that comes from his own pocket though the company pays for him.

Not ten years ago people were deriding Vancouver property and now look. Surely Prince Rupert property will be a success. The only real damper would be a war between England and Germany and personally I can hardly see how that could be. Of course we are so far from current news (I've had only one paper three weeks old, two days ago) and our magazines are American so I may be at fault in my judgment.

A very bright little Englishman a Mr. Pierce, government engineer, was here the other day. He said that such a war would so depopulate both England and Germany. He said, "I don't want to see my relatives cleaned out like so many rabbits."

Do tell me about the political situation at home.

I hoped this would go out in the mail sack but I think Shorty has gone.

With bushels of love to you all, I am just yours the same,
Bernice

The Boo family who lived near Decker Lake in an area today known as Boo Flats. *Bulkley Valley Museum, P509*

The Boos

The Boo family was of the Wet'suwet'en First Nation. In 1912, the identified family members were Donald Boo, Lucy Boo, Sarah Boo and Leon (or Leno) Boo.

At the time of construction of the Grand Trunk Pacific Railway this Wet'suwet'en family, and essentially all of the First Nations, were being greatly impacted by massive cultural change. The influx of settlers brought negative influences: alcohol, residential schools, the reserves and the banning of potlatches. First Nations are still feeling the effects of this today.

As is evidenced in Bernice's letters the Boo family continued their seasonal rounds and their traditional lifestyle. She refers to First Nations men leaving their construction of the Foley, Welch and Stewart cache, seemingly abandoning their jobs as soon as autumn arrived, and she refers to the Boo women making use of the animal skins and sinew.

Sir Donald Boo, Lady Lucy Boo, an unnamed young woman, and little Leonard (a.k.a. Leno and Leon) Boo. *Bulkley Valley Museum, P513*

continued...

Although the Boo surname is no longer in the Decker or Burns Lake area, descendants of this family still live there today. Individuals in Moricetown, Smithers, Prince George, Vancouver and points beyond the Northwest can trace their lineage back to the Decker Lake Boos.

Boo means "wolf" in the Wet'suwet'en language. The area west of Burns Lake is commonly referred to as Boos Flats. Boo Mountain and Boo Lake west of Burns Lake were also named for them.

DECKER LAKE
WEDNESDAY, OCT. 9, 1912

My Dear Marjorie,

Your wire came up today—bless the whole lot of you.

Yesterday Leslie was busy at the office all day; I ironed and baked a cake, made cocoa and sandwiches. Then I went for Les. About 4:30 we started back for the road. There is a thin trail for a quarter mile to where we struck the main government trail. That is a trail, almost a road, along which the telegraph is strung and which was at one time the only avenue into the country. The hills are small with birch, alder, cottonwood and a bit of fir following the course of a tiny stream. We crossed the government trail and sat down in a hollow to sandwiches. Right out of the bush a great big hoot owl remarked "who's who." Every time we spoke to him he cocked his head at a different angle and hooted. We shouted with laughter.

Sunday the beautiful Foley, Welsh, and Stewart tug took her first trip down the lakes. Les was going with Mr. Luck, who built her and LaRouque, who is to run her for the rest of the season. Leslie did not want me to go. I told him he was being silly and selfish and then he said, "Well, come along." Then I wouldn't go. Listen to any pair of ten year olds and you would get the idea. In the end he buttoned my dress and carried my steamer rug and off we went.

The lake is long and narrow with long graceful curved shores—8 mile Decker, on to the thoroughfare and then we did only 8 miles of Burns. There is a bridge in one place where the government is opening a road into some new country near Frances Lake. We passed the hospital, just getting into shape for work over these 100 miles. Then we passed Dan Stewart's Camp, a big job with three camps. Then it is the engineer's camp, and then our camps one and two. One is on a hill among the loveliest trees, a little stream, and pretty cabins. We had dinner there then went down to camp two, home to about six cabins. I wish I could make you see the sunshine, the yellow leaves and the long peaceful lake.

Send me a box of hairpins, 25 cents, large size. If it is not a dollar's worth there is no duty. There are no hairpins in Rupert and you are as close as anybody. Though I did have a Hazelton store buy me some lovely woollen underwear and sent to Simpson's for a housecoat for Leslie.

Good night, sweet dream and my heart's best love,

Bernice

⟶

D.A. RANKIN AND CO. OFFICE
DECKER LAKE
OCTOBER 10, 1912

My dear big sister,

When they built the cabin they hewed bark off one side of the logs, all the chips were left where they fell. Today Leslie set them on fire. I can hardly see for the smoke stung my eyes when I was fixing the bread.

Someone shot rabbits, Frank Bowness brought them over. Monty Johnson skinned them and I will cook them. We will have quite a dinner party.

You have no idea the cost of living up here. A man stayed two days in Aldermere. His bill was $10 and his team was $22. The rate of travel is a dollar a mile by wagon road for one person, and the distance anywhere is fifty miles. Two bales of hay sold for $27 here last week. I notice the Fondy papers quote potatoes at $1.15 to $1.50 a bushel, I wonder what they would say to $15 for a small bushel.

—

This is now days later. Mr. and Mrs. Sprauge arrived. She is the woman I stayed with at Residency 35 for two weeks. Her husband is the assistant (meaning assistant to the chief engineer of construction) of the western division of the GTP and inspector of nine or ten resident engineers. His work lies through here and down past our work on Burns Lake.

Mrs. Sprauge will be with me a week or more until her cabin is finished. I am so glad to have her. American—says "summah" and does a beautiful Irish crochet.

Love love,

Bernice

⟶

DECKER LAKE
OCTOBER 19, 1912

My dearest Mother,

Finishing a house over one's head is said to be the most rapid but there are rapids and rapids.

In the course of two weeks: the storehouse shelves are in the kitchen, the china closet shelves, the table, and all the knives, forks and egg beaters are hanging in place. There is a wood box and two pails of water. We have a chiffonier for Leslie and a washstand. All boxes are covered with unbleached factory to hide the rough boards. The stove, my trunk, our dining table of natural wood with pole legs, our little table, chairs and two couches complete the picture.

—

The bed is made, the ceiling wiped, the clock dried and the mirror wiped off. The cabin has been sweating since the fire is hot and the drips drop, most of them go down my back. In the bedroom they hang suspended in the ceiling cloth. The wood we are burning is only half dry.

Praise be! Our house was banked yesterday. Edward Haak the barn boss and warehouse man did the work. He dug a fine even little ditch all around the house to get dirt to bank, now I am surrounded by a moat. At present any daring knight who would enter my castle must leap the draw.

—

Yesterday B.B. Kelliher, the chief construction engineer for the whole GTP and Mr. Van Arsdol, the engineer on this end of the work, and two others came in to spend the night. They were put in the office. I caught only a glimpse, four rain coats and four soft hats. They had come over the whole line, boat, saddle etc., just however the trail provided. They came by boat and went on by carriage to Prince Rupert.

Today the *Conveyor*, D.A. Rankin and Company's new boat, made a trip from D.A. Rankin camp, where she was built, up here to the cache. They will load with freight and go down in the morning. She is some boat—a flat-bottomed scow with painted bow and sassy little gasoline engine.

We cut a couple of circles in the boat and then I had them to dinner. We were four around the table, Les and I and Mr. Luck, one of the D.A. Rankin Co. men in charge of three camps and Mr. LaRoque, the boatman. I served veal from a can, cabbage salad, peaches, cake and coffee.

Days are never lonesome or idle. True, I am the only woman here but there have been plenty of women about me all my days, so present conditions do not bother me. In a week or ten days the portly Mrs. Sheehan will be here and in six weeks Mrs. Bowness and the little girls.

Les brought the family Boo over one day and showed them our big marble clock. He hopes to trade it to Boo for a bearskin or two.

Now I must go to bed.

With bushels of love from your fly-fighting daughter,

Bernice

DECKER LAKE
TUESDAY, OCTOBER 22, 1912

My dearest Mother,

Blindman's holiday. Six, the clock just struck.

Leslie has gone into Sealey, near Skeena Crossing, perhaps way down to Hardscrabble. It is only a little over a hundred miles to Sealey but it has to be driven and even with a driving team it takes four days.

The mail addressed to Aldermere is put in a sack and taken out here every other week by one of the freight teams. One teamster was drunk and left his sack at South Bulkley, a telegraph station not a town, but the next man brought it on through.

Patience in matters of that sort is the common attitude of all the railroaders.

All day the men have been chopping trees and with two horses dragging them by the house. This gang of ten or more has taken the place of the Indian chief who had the contract for building the Foley, Welch and Stewart cache. Old Chief Wad-hel-da-le could not do the work because with the winter coming he just could not get his men to stay. Those two buildings are 200 ft long by 4 ft wide.

Mr. Bowness has a gang working on his roadhouse, barn and his own house.

Doc Sheehan left the country yesterday. He and his flunkeys had been drunk for almost three weeks. No one had collected from his boarders so his cook left him. He had almost 20 men for meals. His wife is the backbone and she is not here.

Yesterday we had our first flurry of snow. It was light and wet and not much of it. Drip, drip, drip. The house is sweating and the spatters on the carpet sound hollow. We have a log floor just hollowed off with a broadaxe. The cabin is almost finished. We must stuff paper around the chinks of the window in the bedroom.

Just now we have plenty of root vegetables. Our own canned fruit has just given out. The fruit supplied is only dried figs and peaches. The figs are wonderful.

I have joined the catalogue buyers. Ordered felt-lined shoes and fleece-lined stockings. My chilblains have shown up and I am planning to get the best of them. Bushels of love,

Bernice

WAITING FOR LESLIE TO COME TO BREAKFAST
TUESDAY, OCTOBER 29

Dearest Mother,

Last Thursday I had a fine start on a letter to you when Ed called me to the phone to talk to Leslie. That phone is a blessing that we did not have at Hardscrabble. The line is direct from here to Barrett's Cache, and from there connects with Aldermere, then New Hazelton (contract and engineer's headquarters) and thence to Sealey. Sealey was the shipping point for a long time but now that the RR is in New Hazelton the swings only have to go that far. The trip from New Hazelton to Sealey is only five miles but it is over the worst road I ever saw. Soft mud, water, roots and stumps, that with hundreds of horses going over it every day and almost all dragging great heavy wagons, has made it fierce.

Leslie had phoned from Aldermere not knowing whether he had to go back to Hazelton, some 56 miles or not for D.A. Rankin. But D.A. Rankin had arranged to come out with another contractor, Johnnie Albi, so Les came on.

The second day he drove 50 miles and just after I had gone to bed I heard a gent whistling toward the house, tramp on the portcullis and up to the door. I was surprised and entirely delighted. We gossiped and giggled and exchanged news items for an hour.

Bernice Martin and unidentified friend on a horse-drawn cutter. Decker Lake.

Bulkley Valley Museum, P2854

—

The colony grows apace. There is a cabin and three tents for the crew building the Foley, Welch and Stewart cache. The cache buildings themselves are going up. The Bowness's house is up and all ready except a permanent roof. His root cellar is nearly finished and his roadhouse is well started. Our outfit is in good condition.

Today I baked and scratched about. About noon I went to the office and found Mr. Paddy Ryan, the Foley, Welch and Stewart paymaster and Dr. Park, the resident RR doctor from Barrett's Cache. They came to lunch: baked ham, canned corn, scalloped potatoes. I cut up three old baked ones and chucked them under the others when I discovered they were coming. Milk to drink.

—

Les bought me a .22 Winchester for my birthday and I bet there won't be another grouse up here this winter.

—

Mr. D.A. Rankin and the faithful Edward arrived and they were here for supper, Mr. Bowness too. The extra table had to be drawn up to hold the lamp and the hard sauce was so hard it broke the spoon but it was fun.

Mr. D.A. Rankin is a big fat sandy-haired man, charming soft voice and pleasant smile, 42 years old and involved in a half-dozen RR building contracts such as this.

This letter has dragged on for nearly a week and I feel now that I have not said a word. Here it is 10:30 and Les is going to bed, he has filled the stove. The little airtight keeps the fire going all night.

Good night. Bushels of love,
Bernice

WINTER 1912-13

"I have done nothing but cook,
men coming and going. Les brings them
for a meal or two. So it goes. I nearly
wept a tear when I heard I was to have
neighbors, right near—women!"

For most of November 1912, the bridge building gang waited impatiently at Mud Creek for the necessary steel to arrive. The extended delay in the construction materials meant the Mud Creek crossing was not completed until January 1913. The bridge building gang moved up the grade to Porphry Creek and the track-laying crew followed. That month a large concrete crew worked on the foundation and piers at Trout Creek trying to get well ahead of the bridge building gang. In March, the bridge at Porphry Creek was completed and this became the winter end of line for the work trains. Shadey and Paget abandoned their camp at Porphry Creek and the GTP took over the camp as its freight terminal buildings.

The tunnel construction east of New Hazelton moved the grade past a canyon in the Bulkley River by cutting through a mountainside. Three tunnels were built within six miles (ten kilometres); one was the longest on the entire route at 2,214 feet (675 metres) long and was worked at from both ends. A gang of twenty men were moved to the site to build bunkhouses, a mess hall and offices for the two hundred men lining the three tunnels with concrete. Bates and Rogers had the concrete contract

ABOVE: The pick and shovel road-building gang working near Smithers. *Bulkley Valley Museum, P0127*

for all the tunnels and moved their portable plants and men from tunnel to tunnel. It was very slow work. The timbers holding the walls and roof were taken out one or two at a time while the tunnels were lined.

By January 1913, the contracts for grading the railway right-of-way between South Hazelton and Telkwa were well underway. Clearing the right-of-way was hard work. Despite having the steam shovels, donkey engines and dump cars, the majority of clearing was done by men using hand tools and wheelbarrows. Contracts for filling the massive swamp at the base of Hudson Bay Mountain for the Smithers rail yard, roundhouse and station were in progress. There was a camp of almost two hundred men near Chicken Lake working on the grade near the lake and farther east through the future Smithers townsite.

The movement of heavy equipment was best done in winter and contractors all along the right-of-way made use of the snow and hired large horse teams and experienced freighters to haul donkey engines, disassembled steam shovels and locomotives on their sleds. Progress was slow despite strong horses and good hauling conditions. It took nine days to haul Mr. Bostrom's steam shovel from Aldermere to Decker Lake. Work on clearing and levelling the railway right-of-way demanded lots of men and, if a contractor could get them, steam shovels.

Horses proved a wise investment and every able-bodied man with a horse and sleigh offered his services hauling freight. Rates were high. All supplies went to Decker Lake where they were hauled across the frozen lakes to the various construction camps at Burns Lake and Fraser Lake. In the winter of 1912–13 Bernice and Leslie must have witnessed hundreds of horses travelling to and from Decker Lake.

Johnny Albi returned to Decker Lake with twenty horses after a holiday in Spokane. A. Sibbitt brought in four coal-black horses from Portland, Orgeon, and freighted between Aldermere and Decker Lake. The Hazelton *Omenica Miner* stated that at least one hundred horses hauled local freight near Hazelton and more than one thousand hauled out of Hazelton to the Bulkley Valley and Decker Lake. A twenty-eight-mile (forty-five-kilometre) sleigh road over the ice of Burns Lake to Stella on Fraser Lake was very busy; supplies shipped over the road totalled eleven thousand pounds (five thousand kilograms) by the end of January. Stages also did good business.

Frank Carel invested in a high-quality wagon and heavy horses he intended to put to use once the snow disappeared.

Winter brought snowslides to the newly constructed line and a train never left nor arrived on time. Where slides occurred frequently, men hastily constructed snowsheds to protect the track and the accompanying telegraph line. Delays were often very long because men from the nearest camp had to walk or if they were lucky ride on a work train to the site of the slide to clear all the heavy snow away by hand.

Construction continued through the winter and if rocks or frozen earth blocked the progress of the tracks then the men turned to blasting. Heavy rock work took place at the Stewart Brothers' contract at Decker Lake. In March 1913, the manager of Stewart Brothers, Dick Johnson, set off the biggest blast in the history of the construction of the GTP. The explosion demolished a mountain of rock on the shore and heaved up the ice in a reef clear across the lake. Over fifty-two tons of black powder and five tons of dynamite were used.

There were fatalities along the line but Bernice does not write home about the accidents that occurred, perhaps not wanting to worry her family. Slides killed two workers and another two were killed by falling frozen earth. An accident occurred in January at the Stewart Brothers Camp near Burns Lake; men were unloading a kyote that had failed to go off and somehow the powder was ignited. The explosion threw three men two hundred feet (sixty metres) out of the hole and killed them instantly. Many more men were injured in the winter due to accidents involving explosives than any other time of the year.

Labourers were hard to retain and the GTP announced it wanted one thousand new men to be rushed to the Bulkley Valley for work. Captain McLeod made a special trip to Aldermere and tried to recruit a dozen good "rock men."

During the winter of 1912, the Department of Labour conducted an inquiry into camp conditions along the line. The investigation took place east of Fort George and revealed that in some camps men were asked to work off the expense of their clothing, boots and bedding. This resulted in some men working for "free" for a lengthy time before ever seeing any money come to them. The Department of Labour promised they would continue to investigate the situations in the camps along the line.

Winter was a good time for contractors to transport heavy freight. Horses bear the weight, pulling Foley, Welch and Stewart's equipment through Aldermere en route to eastern contracts. *Bulkley Valley Museum, P0523*

The winter brought another challenge to workers along the line in the form of their pay cheques. Labourers who worked along the line were issued time cheques, showing the number of hours worked and their wages earned. Businesses along the line accepted these time cheques as cash until Foley, Welch and Stewart announced in November 1912 that cashing time cheques and station men's estimates was prohibited except at the official pay offices of the company. At this time, the nearest official pay office was in New Hazelton and this meant a long winter walk or expensive sleigh fare for workers to secure the cash for their time cheques. Labourers and businesses were unhappy and demanded that Foley, Welch and Stewart issue subsidiary pay offices all along the line. For two long winter months, labourers and most store owners petitioned for change. In January 1913, Foley, Welch and Stewart relented and lifted the ban on cashing time cheques and sent a paymaster along the line once a month to collect time cheques and issue bank cheques. There were hundreds of men working at D.A. Rankin's camp and other camps along Burns and Decker lakes. Such was the volume of work that in February, Foley, Welch and Stewart moved their pay offices and headquarters to Decker Lake.

A rough winter cabin. Note the canvas roof and bent stovepipe. *Bulkley Valley Museum, P0501*

Before the snow roads thawed, Superintendent Sheppard, D.A. Rankin, John W. Stewart and John Retalick made a record trip along the grade from Hazelton to Fort George. They travelled 300 miles (482 kilometres) in six days with a strong sleighing team to inspect the "gap" in construction between Fraser Lake and Fort George. Their travelling speed would become difficult to believe in just a few months when the roads turned to miles of mud.

Completion of the line came closer to a reality and John W. Stewart of Foley, Welch and Stewart announced the letting of the contracts covering the "gap," the last 140-mile (225-kilometre) section of land between Fraser Lake and Fort George. Contracts varied in length from five to thirty miles (eight to forty-eight kilometres).

Decker Lake grew as businesses previously located near Hazelton closed up shop and moved to this next staging point. One entrepreneurial blacksmith, Gus Dahr, opened a shop at Decker Lake with several tons of steel on hand and sent out for a lighting system so he could run his shop day and night. Boat builders moved to Decker Lake knowing that when the snow roads over Burns and Decker lakes broke up in the spring, there would be a steady demand for boats to haul construction materials and men. Bob Gerow and Mr. Laidlaw established a sawmill at Decker Lake and could not keep up with the demand for lumber. Bernice must have welcomed the influx of new settlers as Decker Lake grew and new buildings went up.

DECKER LAKE
SUNDAY, NOVEMBER 3, 1912

Good afternoon Mrs. Ruthie Devoin,
Les will go into Hardscrabble, load the outfit onto the train, get it to New Hazelton and see it loaded on wagons or sleighs, to come out here. Les asks me if I want to come. If I am in Hazelton for three weeks I will take a run to Rupert.

For two weeks I have done nothing but cook, men coming and going. Les brings them for a meal or two. So it goes. I nearly wept a tear when I heard I was to have neighbors, right near—women!

Weather—one delightful fall, not a blemish in it. They say it is raining like H--- in Rupert.
A bushel of love to you and Manford.
Your baby sister,
Bernice

DECKER LAKE
WEDNESDAY, NOVEMBER 6, 1912

My dear Mother,
Today I washed the floor. You would have a fit to see it, clean as it is. Poles, adzed off on one side only. You can guess the size of the cracks in between. It is a tossup whether the advantage of sweeping all the dirt into the cracks or the disadvantage of losing anything smaller than a teacup is greater.

I am going to Hazelton with Leslie for three weeks, about two weeks from now.

Mrs. Bowness and one of the "little Bowness girls" with Lady Lucy Boo, Decker Lake. *Bulkley Valley Museum, P2850*

It will give me a splendid trip.

When D.A. Rankin buys beef, Bobby Grant, the local agent for P. Burns, rides in with his herd of cattle. A man picks out the one that suits, loads his gun and ends Mr. Beef. The meat we get, the hide is strung on a pole to be collected later and the rest the Indian women cart off. They wash the internal workings and use them for some such thing.

Leslie and the cat Smutty are asleep on the sofa, I must shoo them off to bed. My bestest love to my deary mother,

Bernice

DECKER LAKE VIA ALDERMERE
NOVEMBER 13, 1912

My dear Marjorie,

We are sitting here quietly with Mr. and Mrs. Bowness. Leslie is reading and I am with you. Their three, four and five-year-old girls are staying here for a week or so. Last night we had a good hand of whist. Will again tomorrow.

The last of this week Les and I are going to Hazelton, 4 or 5-day trip and, as we are to go on wheels, it may be a hard trip. Come back by sleigh.

Anything you send right through by mail, address Decker Lake via Aldermere. We are to have a post office right here one day. The Burns Lake address carries them by and they are ages coming back. If you do send express send it to me or Les c/o Mrs. S.E. Parker. Then express to Hazelton or New Hazelton and then freight out here, all of which means, to be successfully carried out, trouble for someone, to say nothing of expense.

Morning light just starts at 7 and it is dark at 5:30 or earlier.

I am half asleep, worse luck is the company that will eat three times a day, drat it. Mrs. Bowness is fine to help about things. Always sets the table and wipes the dishes. Her kids are as cute as can be.

Bushels of love to you both,

Bernice

Hubert and Smithers

Hubert was once a sparsely populated community on the west side of the Bulkley River, upstream from Telkwa. Brave settlers had purchased and painstakingly cleared large sections of flat land in hopes that the Grand Trunk Pacific Railway would focus on Hubert as the ideal spot for the divisional point. Grand Trunk Pacific Railway officials were silent on where their large roundhouse and railway buildings would go. People knew that where the roundhouse went, an instant boom town would soon follow. The selection of a divisional point in the railway would guarantee services for residents, sales for new businesses and provide a market for farmers. Speculation was rampant.

There were not many flat sites in the Bulkley Valley and there were only two that also allowed for a long section of straight tracks; either the swampy land at the foot of Hudson Bay Mountain or the pioneer farming community of Hubert. When land surveyors were spotted in Hubert, people became sure Hubert was the next big city. Aldermere's *Interior News* referred to Hubert as the only "big city development" between Prince Rupert and Fort George.

In March 1913, Land Commissioner G. Ryley made an announcement that spelled the sudden end of the community of Hubert.

As stated in the *Daily News Advertiser* of Vancouver, the Board of Railway Commissioners in Ottawa "...approved the station site of Smithers, the second divisional point east of Prince Rupert, Mile 226.5 on the Grand Trunk Pacific Railway about 9 miles west of Telkwa and Aldermere. The townsite will be for sale in August 1913 and Messrs. Aldous and Murray, Hazelton, have been appointed agents for the sale of lots. It is expected that the plan of the townsite and prices of the lots will be ready for distribution in July."

Citizens of Aldermere, Telkwa and Hubert were surprised. Some businesses in Hubert relocated to the wet ground of Smithers and hardy settlers put up canvas tents to live in. Few had suspected the railway company would choose the swampy section of land at the base of Hudson Bay Mountain as a divisional point.

Smithers was named for the chairman of the board of directors of the Grand Trunk Pacific Railway, Sir Alfred Waldron Smithers.

Horse-drawn dump carts helped ease the physical labour of the men. They were used to make a fill and build a level rail grade. Here they are being used to fill in the Smithers swamp. *Bulkley Valley Museum, P0218*

DECKER LAKE VIA ALDERMERE
FEBRUARY 1, 1913

My dearest Mother and Father,
After begging for fresh vegetables for weeks, Les arranged for Mickey to bring 25 pounds each of all different kinds he could find. One box of apples lasts us exactly a month. We ate them up like so much candy. But they were worth it.

Alma Ross and I have just been for a grand walk, away down the lake to a marsh where there is a trestle built on which the donkey cars will run out and dump dirt into the marsh filling it till it becomes part of the grade or ground over which the rails are laid.

Next we crossed the trestle and followed the shore and started to step right on the road. We saw where snowshoes had gone and we followed dropping right through the crust every few steps not quite knee deep. Our walk home was only 20 minutes.

The day is clear and all day stray snowflakes have been drifting down. Eight minutes

The McInnes Ranch

"Pioneer Ranch" McInnes Bros owner

Brothers Archie and Neil McInnes came to British Columbia from Ontario in 1883. They led a typical roving pioneer lifestyle; they worked for the Douglas Lake Cattle Company, they mined at Manson Creek and they helped in the building of the Dominion Telegraph Line north out of Hazelton.

From 1901 to 1904 Archie and Neil lived and worked at the North Bulkley telegraph cabin, near present-day Perow. They loved the area so much they pre-empted their farm at North Bulkley in 1904 calling it the Pioneer Ranch. Archie married Jessie and they had three daughters, Vera, Ivy and Neva. Archie and Jessie and "Uncle Neil" farmed the Pioneer Ranch until 1946. Neil died in Terrace in 1948 and Archie died also in Terrace in 1951. Descendants of Archie and Jessie live in the area today.

Tie Hackers

All wooden railway ties were hand hewn. Trees were felled, cut, surfaced with a broadaxe and dragged to a convenient staging spot. Walter Wicks wrote that, "tie hackers received six cents per tie, which for an average of sixty ties per ten-hour day gave them a day's wages of $3.60."

The demand for railway ties was such that large temporary tie camps were established close to the necessary forest and near enough to the railway siding. The 1911 census lists hundreds of men employed as "axeman."

Tie cutting also provided winter employment for many of the pioneer farmers along the Grand Trunk Pacific construction line.

A large pile of hand-hewn railway ties for use on the construction of the Grand Trunk Pacific. *Bulkley Valley Museum, P0273*

before five and the thermometer is at 24 Fahrenheit. That is above of course. If this lasts much longer the snow road will be broken up. The shortcuts across the many little lakes are all broken up now.

Last week Dick Johnson, the manager for Stewart Brothers, brought in their second shovel and I got some splendid pictures of them.

On the 12th the McInnes' are having a housewarming. Skookum Johnson is coming up here with Johnny Ateams to take down a load. You see here is Alma Ross, the only unmarried girl in 100 miles and it won't due to not have her at a party. Skookum is the resident engineer at 34 mile, next to Ehlrich's where I stayed, and he is only a mile or less from McInnes'.

McInnes and his brother were telegraph linemen and are now ranchers. Also Mrs. McInnes's brother, whose name I just forgot. She is the woman who started for the stork, started for the hospital and got caught at roadhouse mile 20. It's run by Black Jack McDonald and is just what it sounds and she, the sweetest English girl. She has as a friend and housekeeper a Miss Booth. It has been the subject of much local gossip as to whether his brother or her brother would win the fair lady. Hers won out. Well, we are all invited to the ball. If all goes well we will take Mrs. Sprauge, Skooke will take Alma and possibly Mrs. Bowness. Mrs. Ross won't go because it is a party. You see her husband has not been dead quite two years, oh ye Canadians. This party means a drive down one day, dance and romp all night and drive back the next day, only 31 miles.

Now I will envelope this in case Paddy Ryan is going early in the morning he will take it.

Bushels of love,

Bernice

⚬

DECKER LAKE
FEBRUARY 14, 1913

Mother, Father, Marjorie and Chauncey,

Here I am married a year and am still as happy, as fat and as sassy as I was before I walked down the drawing room and was kissed by a very red faced husband and a mob of friends.

Sir Donald Boo and Lady Lucy brought their child to Bernice to photograph as the infant was very ill with a fever and they worried she might die. *Bulkley Valley Museum, P508*

Out here life on the whole pivots around the RR work and its people. They are different from any group I have met before and they are arranged in groups within groups and here at the end of one year I am an ignoramus on the subject.

Well I want to tell you about this week's doings. Wednesday about 9 am Mr. and Mrs. Bowness, Alma Ross, Jack Green and Skookum Johnson, who had come up with a bob sleigh, took the party down to the McInnes' for a housewarming party. We had decided to stay home and do washing. It had been cold and we had had company, or Les had, men on business, so we had three week's accumulation.

But we had finished the washing by noon and Les said he would hitch up the cayuses and we would go down for Mrs. Sprauge, if I wanted to go to McInnes' party. Of course, I left the dishes in the pan, changed my waist and shoes and we started.

I wore Leslie's moccasins over my shoes, my red cap, brown coat over a hug-me tight vest. Off we drove to pick up Mrs. Sprauge.★

Passed a couple of bohunks who tumbled off the road to let us pass with the words, "How'sh chances for a ride Leslie?" Of course nothing doing. Then up off Decker Lake onto the land to pass by the thoroughfare between two lakes and then past the

★EDITOR'S NOTE: *They would have had to travel eastward to Burns Lake to pick up Mrs. Sprauge then back westward, past their home at Decker Lake and on to the McInnes' farm.*

McKenna roadhouse and ranch. Then past the Indian village, then the trail leads to the left a quarter mile to the Burns Lake telegraph station and post office, next to the hospital.

Well just through a little clump of cedars around the hospital we passed a bunch of Indians. Team of cayuses with one load including papa, mama and baby. The prettiest Indian baby I have ever seen, placidly breakfasting as they rode along. The road was narrow for a team so Les drove over. The Indian lifted the end of the double tree off our team, then moved on. Our team climbed nimbly down and off we went with a pleasant how de do. Next came the kids, two little girls of five or six with two young women of 17 or 20 and a man trailing them and a puppy and a dog hitched to a loaded wagon. A bit farther two big huskies and grandmother plodding along. Well, we got to the Spragues' and she packed a suitcase while we had tea. Then we started back to the party.

———

This is a gorgeous day. All sunshine but it may honeycomb the ice if we have much more of it.

———

The GTP Steamship Service

The Grand Trunk Pacific needed to transport railway building materials, men and supplies to the western end of construction. Prince Rupert was chosen as the terminus point, the port with an imagined future city. Construction on a wharf on Kaien Island began in spring of 1906. The GTP acquired a tug and barge operation that ran between Vancouver and Prince Rupert in 1908. Construction materials were stockpiled near the Prince Rupert oceanfront.

In 1909 the GTP began steamship service between the Queen Charlotte Islands (now Haida Gwaii) and Prince Rupert. The GTP Coast Steamship Service was incorporated in 1910, and two GTP passenger ships, the SS *Prince Rupert* and the SS *Prince George* provided service between Prince Rupert and the southern cities of Vancouver, Victoria and Seattle.

Ah Jim and Luey, the Bowness roadhouse cook and waiter, father and son, got in a quarrel. Jim said, "You do so and so or I'll kill myself." Luey said in Chinese, "go to it old man." Whereupon Jim started for his abdomen with the largest carver. Luey got to him in time to strike the knife down but Jim got a bad artery cut on his leg. So off to the hospital we carried him.

A bushel of love,

Bernice

WELCOME COTTAGE, DECKER LAKE
MARCH 2, 1913

Dearest Family,

Harris Ross and Jack Green borrowed a cutter from Leslie and hitched a Foley, Welch and Stewart horse to it. After Mrs. Ross had a ride Les and I went up the lake for a spin. The lake road is very fair but the land roads are growing bad. We drove past the Foley, Welch and Stewart powder house and as far as Stewart's tent. Came just as they were going up for their steam shovel crew. They will begin to operate a shovel less than a mile from here. Even Bostrom's shovel has gone through. His work is some 40 or 50 miles east from here.

Decker Lake grows a pace. Four barbers, two blacksmiths, six blind pigs, two stores, one Decker Lake Club and one poolroom.

Campbell's soup sells for 40 cents a can. I am using dehydro things.

Well, I had the nicest surprise yesterday. Mr. Charlie Barrett phoned up to ask Mrs. Ross and Alma, Mrs. Bowness and the kiddies and I to go down to his ranch for a ten-day visit. Mrs. Bowness can't go but we three will. He is one character, an Englishman who has trapped in here for years for the Hudson's Bay Company. His ranch is called by everyone the Home Ranch. His sister was to come but she died instead of coming so he has kept an open house ever since; men always and women and children when he can find them. He wants every man to stop in on his way in or out. Everyone is his friend and he delights in filling his rooms with guests. He has a crackerjack Chinaman and all the joys of farm life. One room upstairs bunks with Hudson's Bay Company blankets, a keg of rye and a keg of Scotch on spigots like water for every visitor. Downstairs are carpets and brass beds. One contractor's camp and one engineer's camp are right on the place. We will have a grand visit and maybe get to Aldermere, our nearest metropolis.

I see the mail stage is in and now I had better take this over myself.

Bernice

Leslie Martin, Mrs. Bowness, two unidentified men and Margaret and Francis Bowness at Decker Lake.
Bulkley Valley Museum P2849

DECKER LAKE, BC

My Dear Ruth,

Friday I returned from a visit to Barrett's ranch and found your letter.

All this time you must have thought me exceedingly unsympathetic. I had no idea Manford had been so badly injured or as sick as it now appears he has been.

All the miles and hours between us—so I use this line of logic. If it is very bad they will let me know by wire. If news comes in a letter it has had a three week trip and the sick person could get well in that time, so I picture the recovered person instead of the injured one.

Next I start for the coast in anticipation of seeing my family. It will be a fearful trip for me. 3 or 4 days of drive in the cold, 200 miles by rail and they expect me to go to Seattle. That will mean 600 miles more and it also means staying out two months. By that time the roads will be impassable so I can't get home.

If I can get them to Rupert I may get back before the last breakup of the roads.

I am off, mail this and cook a steak, the first beef in a week.

Bernice

SPRING 1913

"…the horses plunged ahead. Bang, we hit a rock, bing, I hit the road, flip flop, and robes all spread with mud. The greater part of that mud hole squirted in my ear."

The Grand Trunk Pacific's SS *Prince Rupert. Bulkley Valley Museum, P1942*

Steamers that docked at Prince Rupert in the early spring of 1913 brought a record number of land buyers North who hoped to purchase property before the Grand Trunk Pacific Railway was completed. Many were enticed North by advertisements placed in southern papers by land sellers such as Reginald Gale in Telkwa offering farmland for $9 to $20. Fred Heal, who settled in the Bulkley Valley in 1903, also advertised land for sale, one especially tempting ad read, "$500 for an 80-acre cleared farm." Both buyers and sellers believed that once the GTPR was completed the price of land would greatly increase.

In the spring of 1913 the GTP steamer *Prince Rupert* had a list of 195 first-class passengers. Many saw an opportunity too good to pass up and brought their families and all their belongings North to settle before the prospective boom.

At this time freight and passenger service was approved to travel through South Hazelton and up to New Hazelton. The track was laid past New Hazelton but only work trains rumbled down the tracks to Porphry Creek.

Entrepreneurs such as W.J. "Wiggs" O'Neill, Mr. Bigelow and Mr. McAffee shipped in some of the very first automobiles (a Russell-Knight car and a Packard

Spring floods led to track washouts and mudslides along the line. Here labourers stand beside a mired steam shovel, the pick and shovel gang hard at work.

The Valley Museum and Archives and the Exploration Place, 2003-25-133

Teamsters freighting goods and supplies to the many railroad camps travelled together to help each other out of the mudholes along the telegraph trail route. *Bulkley Valley Museum, P0601*

truck) and advertised transportation to Aldermere and Telkwa from the last passenger stop at New Hazelton. Despite advertisements in the spring newspapers, the auto stages were forced to wait for the road conditions to improve before they jostled their passengers over rough wagon roads to their inland destinations.

In the early spring of 1913, New Hazelton experienced an influx of settlers; nearly one hundred passengers disembarked from the Grand Trunk Pacific's passenger coaches and the town had no place left to put them. Every hotel, rooming house and front room couch was full and every train for two weeks straight brought more people than the town could accommodate. The passenger trains that stopped at New Hazelton brought forty or more fresh railway labourers in and every departing train brought the same number of tired railroaders back out.

Advertisements in the newspapers turned from sleigh bells to seed drills and warm weather turned the wagon roads to mud. At Decker Lake Bernice and Leslie witnessed the spring temperatures thaw the lake roads. Leslie stopped shipping supplies across

Decker Lake with horse-drawn sleighs and started freighting with boats. On Decker Lake, the *Conveyor* benefited from the high freight movement and left Rankin's Wharf on Decker every morning at eight o'clock for camps along Burns Lake. Spring thaws caused a sudden flood near Decker Lake at Johnny Albi's camp. He and his men had to struggle to get all of his horses and outfits up to drier ground.

Spring led to challenges along the line. The track near Hazelton sank five feet (one and a half metres) over a distance of one hundred feet (thirty metres) in one day. The next day, the sinkhole slid down the bank, carrying the siding with it and left over seventy-five feet (twenty-two metres) of main track suspended in the air. Foley, Welch and Stewart brought in a gravel train and a big gang of men. For two days and one long night, the men hustled to repair the track. They brought in a piledriver and sixty-foot (eighteen-metre) piles were driven under the main line.

Piledrivers were used to level the rail grade or build the approach to a creek or canyon crossing. *Bulkley Valley Museum, P0411*

There was also a bridge embankment that gave way as a long gap opened up between the bank and the bridge. The bridge building gang was recruited and a piledriver was also brought in. Twenty more feet (six metres) had to be added to the bridge. And there were some close calls; a slide came down along the Skeena River and narrowly missed a passenger train, hitting the rear vestibule of the hind coach. And a GTP engine "turned turtle" just before crossing Porphry Creek; an engineer hurt a rib but escaped with minor injuries.

Perhaps it was due to the challenge of mud or the increased pace of construction but injuries were occurring all along the line. The railway hospital at Burns Lake took notice and constructed a thirty- by forty-foot (about nine- by twelve-metre) addition.

In April 1913, two special cars were attached to the train at Prince Rupert for a group of officials who came up to inspect the progress of the rails. On board was Captain Nicholson, the general manager of the GTP Steamship Services, W.C.C. Meehan, W.P. Hinton and other officials. But it was spring and their train was delayed due to an inevitable landslide along the Skeena River section. Once they arrived at Hazelton the party went east of New Hazelton just a few miles and returned to stay the night in Hazelton.

Upon his return to Vancouver in May 1913, W.P. Hinton expressed great faith in the future of northern British Columbia and the northern line and stated the GTP would spend several million dollars in the summer of 1913. Included in the plans were additional steamships to serve Prince Rupert.

GTP Chief Engineer B.B. Kelliher and J.W. Stewart also went out to look over the progress of work. The duo travelled from New Hazelton to Decker Lake by horse team, then by boat across Burns and Decker lakes, where a team picked them up and took them on to Fort Fraser. From there the men travelled by canoe and by team to Fort George.

Gravel cars unloaded along the newly constructed line and ballast trains firmed up the track. With improvements made along the existing line the GTPR attempted to coordinate arrivals in Prince Rupert with the departures of their steamships to the southern cities of Vancouver, Victoria and Seattle. People were now able to check their baggage on the New Hazelton train all the way through to their destination of Seattle.

When steamers, trains and conditions allowed, freight could be shipped from Vancouver to New Hazelton in just two days. This record time encouraged residents and they counted on the railway as a timely method of transporting goods. Residents and merchants ordered fresh goods and perishables. Two carloads of horses were brought in for freighting. Farmers began to bring livestock in on the trains. Both new

Doc Sheehan's hotel at Decker Lake. *Bulkley Valley Museum, P2852*

arrivals and long-time pioneer residents saw the importing of goods and animals as a sign of prosperity, an indicator of the area's success, a guarantee of growth.

Burns and Company shipped carloads of cattle along the line to Porphry Creek, where they were driven inland to the various camps along the line. Burns and Company also shipped cattle by rail from the eastern Alberta side to the eastern end of steel near Fort George and drove the cattle west to the camps around Fraser Lake, Burns Lake and Decker Lake.

The first shipments of ore from mines surrounding Hazelton began to be shipped out by railcar from New Hazelton to Prince Rupert then down the Pacific Ocean destined for a smelter in Tacoma. Complaints were voiced that the GTP charged exorbitant freight rates for ore shipment, $6.40 per ton in carloads from New Hazelton to Prince Rupert, a distance of 180 miles (290 kilometres). The GTP was accused of stalling the development of the region. Miners and shareholders said that the GTP should give a reduced rate to ore. They said this would encourage investments in the area and would ultimately increase the use of the GTP. The GTP was accused of "highway robbery" and mine owners were quick to point out that the railcars departing from New Hazelton returned empty to Prince Rupert anyway.

Despite paying the high freight rate for shipping their ore on the GTP from New Hazelton to Prince Rupert, the mines still had reason to celebrate. In 1913 they learned the Tacoma smelter valued their ore anywhere between $117 a ton and $446 a ton.

More roadhouses sprung up to cater to the passing teamsters and roving settlers. Mr. and Mrs. Bill Bailey moved to Decker Lake from New Hazelton and not only built a large thirty-bed rooming house but also erected a large tent for overflow accommodation. Doctor Sheehan built a large addition to his Decker Lake hotel. Mrs. Bowness and her three daughters were frequent visitors to Bernice's cabin while Frank Bowness built an addition to his Traveller's Hotel.

Decker Lake saw more merchants move to its shores in the spring of 1913. W.R. Larkworthy moved his store from Hazelton to Decker Lake and became the postmaster. Pioneer retailers Broughton and McNeil also opened a branch store at Decker Lake as did Mr. Paterson, a former Kitselas pioneer and merchant.

In May, the Boulder Creek Bridge was completed and several loads of steel were brought up the track for the tracklayer. The bridge builders moved up into the Bulkley Valley to the next major obstacle, a low crossing over a 240-foot (73-metre) span across the Telkwa River near the towns of Telkwa and Aldermere. The road builders stepped up their pace of work as the track-laying crews threatened to catch up. The clearing crews finished at Chicken Lake and a big gang of men was rushed in to help finish clear and level the side tracks at the future Smithers site. The track-laying crew was laying two miles (about three kilometres) a day as it progressed towards Moricetown and then headed for Chicken Lake, just west of the future townsite of Smithers.

In the spring of 1913 Bernice travelled from Decker Lake to Prince Rupert and down the coast to Seattle, Washington, to meet with her mother and father. Aboard the steamer travelling south she wrote a letter to her sister recalling a party at Barrett

Ranch. After a two-week visit in Seattle with her family Bernice returned to Prince Rupert, staying with the Parkers and visiting the Ormes. She then travelled inland to Hazelton where the roads were so bad that Leslie could not send for her. After a prolonged visit at the Kerrs in Hazelton, Leslie came for Bernice and they returned to their home at Decker Lake.

Mrs. Al Brown and Mrs. Doc Orme at Decker Lake.
Bulkley Valley Museum, P2858

ABOARD THE SS PRINCE GEORGE
FRIDAY, APRIL 11, 1913
[BERNICE IS WRITING ABOUT HER VISIT
TO THE BARRETT RANCH]

My Dear Ruth,

Now it is after dinner and after Millbank Sound, about an hour of groundswell and no real sea. One really bad patch is the three or four hour crossing of Queen Charlotte Sound, where we are exposed to open sea. Then we get in at night, the trip promises to be flawless. Some man with a nice easy voice is singing "Pink Lady" in the music room.

I want to go back to my Barrett Ranch visit, two weeks I stayed there. There was:

1. Owen Rand, 43, charming smile and lover of company.
2. George Exley, the English bookkeeper, on the water wagon and best possible kind of business man.
3. Gene, the Chinese cook.
4. Michael Shadey, a RR contractor and successful real estate agent, boards at

Barrett's for his contract lies at the floor of the hill.

5. George Barrett, telegraph operator at government ranch otherwise known as Barrett's Cache.
6. Brother Charlie Barrett, young, tall, good-looking and lazy.
7. Harlow, engineer on Residency 28 or 29, spends most of his time anywhere there is something doing.
8. Carter, Harlow's instrument man, another shire of England.
9. Doc Sprawl, doctor by profession engaged in making love to Alma Ross.
10. E. Hoops, Englishman who came into this country eight years ago via Ashcroft and has never seen Prince Rupert.

Mr. Barrett took us (Alma and I) to Aldermere, 24 miles away to a dance and basket social. Boxes sold from $7.50 to $13.50. The nicest part was meeting people. Mrs. Dorreen, wife of the assistant or district engineer, an intellectual sort and a great friend of Mrs. Sprauge. And the Hoops family; two brothers and a sister. We stayed for two nights and the intervening day with Mrs. William.

We had dinner at J. Mason Adam's. He is the druggist who came out from Hazelton this fall. They are Canadian.

Oh, the woods is full of regular people only we must wear a thousand league boots to find them.

We left Aldermere and went back to Barrett's ranch. Coasting downhill by moonlight on a horse-drawn go-devil with Mr. Shadey, Charlie Barrett, Granger, Exley and George Barrett—it was some slide.

The weather fell to 28 below again but we had to get home. We started at 8 am. We drove about 26 miles across the river and out on the Silverthorne flats onto the government road for miles. Then a trip through the woods, across a curve of the river, past Mr. Shadey's rest camp, out over the meadow and up onto the government road. We drew up to Residency 34, Robey's headquarters. Robey, Sprauge, Betts and Dorreen are the four assistant engineers on the works. Here some fellow said, "There's a letter here for you Mr. Barrett." The letter, of course, was a drink of Scotch.

(Our steamer is just now passing through Seymour Narrows at half speed.)

Decker Lake, spring 1913. The widow Mrs. Ross (Alma and Harris's mother), Bernice and Mrs. Sprauge.
Bulkley Valley Museum, P0537

Then Duncan Ross's big camp, and lunch with the timekeeper, Mr. Cannon. There Mr. Barrett changed horses. Alma and I went up and spent a half-hour with Mrs. Ehlrich where I was for those long weeks last summer.

The trip from there is 24 miles and the team Mr. Barrett was driving is the ruin of a splendid driving team. They started off at a lope, just tearing; all Mr. Barrett could do to hold ground. If Mr. Sprauge had not been ahead I think they would have bolted with us. After ten miles of up and down hills we struck Bulkley Lake, 10 miles down its center.

On Bulkley Lake lies Captain McLeod's work. He is one of the quaintest men up here. He has done some splendid work but is no railroader.

Oh, the wind and sun! I pulled my toque right down over my face for the trip through woods and marsh then Summit Lake. The summit of the RR and the new GTP engineers headquarters. Across from that is Paget's work camp, a group of tent buildings on a flat and near the work.

After Paget's we were on the rise again till Robertson's Roadhouse was passed. Then out onto Boos Flats, the place of the greatest snowfall between Ashcroft and Hazelton. Next through pines, then the cottonwood hill then home.

Tony the dog and Leslie were both so glad to see me. He had had the floor all taken up and laid flat and had the Chinaman come clean house.

I did a big wash, cleaned my gloves, red kimono, blue shirtwaist etc. Did ironing and bread.

Bushels of love

Bernice

HOTEL PERRY, SEATTLE, WASHINGTON
APRIL 15, 1913

My Dear Ruth

Here we are in Seattle and the family looks good to me. At present writing we are all tired and sniffly. Certainly I will try to bring them up the coast with me to Prince Rupert if I can.

We will shop tomorrow for I need a few garments.

This hotel is in town and quite nice.

When this visit is over I will go back to the woods, back to the mines.

Bushels of love,

Bernice

NEW HAZELTON
WEDNESDAY, MAY 21, 1913

[BERNICE'S TRIP HOME TO DECKER LAKE AFTER VISITING HER FAMILY IN SEATTLE]

My dearest Mother,

Here I am at the Kerrs' and Leslie started for me this morning, but the roads are just dreadful. Les wired me to stay, they are so bad. Next thing is when can he get me out?

The trip up the coast to Prince Rupert was grand. We were out playing shuffle board all across Queen Charlotte Sound, where it is supposed to be rough.

I spent a week with Mrs. Parker in Prince Rupert. We had a good visit and saw the movies and had a lot of good food. I made her a nightgown and a housedress. The Parkers are great fun. She tells him to head in and if he does not she gets mad, then he smiles and she gets madder, and then they have it out. I enjoy watching them spar.

The Ormes are fine and their boy of three months weighs 18 pounds, I never saw such fat cheeks.

The day I came up was gorgeous, oh why didn't you come this far? Talk about scenery.

The Kerrs are fine; their baby is gaining flesh and looks like dad.

When Les gets nearer I will talk to him on the phone and then write you again. I suppose he will be here Sunday.

Bushels of love,

Bernice

DIAMOND D RANCH
THURSDAY, MAY 29, 1913

My Dearest Mother,

We had been in Aldermere the night and had to wait until ten in the forenoon to have our horses shoed. Then we drove out with a phonograph, record, shoebox, a pound of tea between us, my feet on a box of greens, suitcases under the big seat and a rooster tied on behind the box. Then we tried to make Popcorn Kate's for lunch. She is one of the characters of the country and I was tickled to think Les was going to take me there. But he niggled before we got there. He found a new place just started, tents in the yard, wash basins on stumps. The meat was a little strong, dumpling, potatoes, gravy, but she had a huckleberry pie.

Then on a few miles and we had to drive through a succession of mud holes up to the hubs and when we thought we were to the last pull the horses plunged ahead, bang, we hit a rock, bing, I hit the road, flip-flop, and robes all spread with mud. The greater part of that mud hole squirted in my ear. I walked up to the top of the hill and climbed in.

Just then Dr. Wallace and his sister-in-law, Miss Libman, came up on their horses and caught me, mud from top to toe.

I got out at the sawmill and Mrs. Roxby (she wears the trousers in that place) took

Roadhouses

Bulkley Valley Museum, P1039

Roadhouses were established along the wagon roads and pack trails to take advantage of the long roads, the slow pace of travel and the scores of men. Some called themselves roadhouses, like Alex Michel's goods store and roadhouse at Moricetown in 1912, offering "Meals—fifty cents, Bed—fifty cents." Some were referred to as rooming houses, like Frank Bowness's hotel at Van Arsdol, offering a bunk and serving only ham and eggs and coffee twenty-four hours a day.

Kate Morrison, "Popcorn Kate," ran a roadhouse between Aldermere and Barrett Ranch, where the Quick district is today. "Popcorn Kate" was known to have a large barn for horses,

continued...

to charge $1.50 for a plate of beans and baking powder biscuits (no butter) and was rumoured to have operated a blind pig (illegal liquor establishment) serving pure alcohol coloured brown with tobacco juice.

The state of the roadhouses varied widely. There were some proprietors who charged fifty cents for a bed, fifty cents for sheets and fifty additional cents if you wanted your sheets to be clean. Others offered "private beds" for the lone woman traveller, which consisted of a sheet pinned around a bunk bed in a room full of bunk beds stacked three levels high. It is easy to understand why Bernice was made to wait for an escort or for Leslie before travelling on the pioneer trails. But thankfully there were a few roadhouses that had good reputations, genial hosts, clean beds, and wholesome meals for the weary traveller and the horses alike.

me to her room, brought hot water, washcloths and towels. I cleaned up a little. Had my big raincoat and that saved the day. I was shaken up of course but not hurt a bit. Today I suggested that I get a baby strap and tie myself in. Mrs. Roxby gave me a cup of tea and we came on.

At the cache, government ranch, we picked up old Mrs. Smith and came on here. It has been raining here for days.

The weather promises to be the worst for roads today and then fairly good home. Leslie just phoned home and Doc said it was pouring up there.

Mr. Barrett went off and Les would not go till he returned. We are staying on until tomorrow then. Just as well because besides the throw, I had the pip and was glad of a day off.

There are new pigs, kittens etc. here. Mr. Barrett has put in a series of irrigation ditches from a dammed-up lake back in the hills a way.

Barrett has his yard inside a nice picket white fence all levelled up and rolled for a lawn. Some things are up in the hot beds but only radishes and lettuce in the open.

There is a bear over in the cache and every day the men go out and hunt. No one gets the bear. It makes for lively conversation around here.

This evening Mr. Barrett is going to brand cattle and I will see it.

Later at home—the house has been cleaned, the windows reset so they will all swing open. Les is great at fixing things up when he gets hungry. This living on beans and ham for six weeks makes him real glad to see me home.

Bushels of love,

Bernice

SUMMER 1913

*"Tell Marj that if she wants
a fellow I'll catch her one. Even the
great, fat Sheppard asked, 'Well, when
is sister coming?'"*

The tracklayer progressing eastward through the Bulkley Valley. *Bulkley Valley Museum, P0002*

I n the summer of 1913 the Skeena River reached its highest level in nine years. The high water levels of the Skeena and Bulkley rivers and their tributary creeks severely tested the railway bridges and cribbing. Trains proceeded slowly over all water crossings and delays were again the norm. The GTP trains carried mail and the mail moved so slowly that residents were receiving no weekly newspapers and then four or five weekly papers at a time.

At the beginning of June, the second tunnel skirting the Bulkley Canyon east of New Hazelton collapsed. Fifty feet (fifteen metres) at one end caved in from the top and contractors Bates and Rogers brought a large crew in to clean it up. So much earth had to be moved that it took almost the entire month.

Dr. Wrinch at the Hazelton hospital was kept very busy with the many broken limbs and crushed feet of those injured along the line. Also in the summer of 1913, Dr. Wrinch made the foreboding announcement of a scarlet fever outbreak and quarantined the affected patients in the hospital at Hazelton.

There were headaches all along the line. The GTP steamer *Prince George* ran aground on a rock outside the Prince Rupert harbour, but fortunately it occurred on a rising tide so the steamer waited one and a half hours and floated off it. Another day an engine tipped off a low level bridge and the derrick, which was brought in to try to pull it out, also tipped over the edge and tumbled down. Also a gin pole derrick was being moved past the depot at New Hazelton when its boom became ensnared in the telegraph wires and it crashed into the depot with such force that the depot was extensively damaged.

Trains leaving New Hazelton heading for Prince Rupert were full of labourers who hoped to find better conditions and wages elsewhere. In Bernice's June letter home she makes her one and only reference to the labour discontent

The bridge building gang reach the Telkwa River. *Bulkley Valley Museum, P0230*

at their Decker Lake Camp by saying, "the laborers camp out; they are independent of a job." Later she states, "Our food supply is alright as far as we personally are concerned." Yet, as before, fresh labourers arrived to replace the worn-out workers.

The tracks constantly progressed and in July the railway granted freight and passenger service to Moricetown. First the grading and piledriving was completed to east of Trout Creek then at the beginning of August, the track-laying crew had passed Chicken Lake, then Chicken Creek and finally Smithers. Mr. Dempsey rushed his tracklayer through the straight stretch at Smithers and on to Telkwa where they were forced to wait for the Telkwa Bridge to be completed. The bridge builders were anxious to get out of Dempsey's way and completed the bridge across the Telkwa River. Soon the rails had been laid across the Telkwa River and in to Hubert.

The GTP Railway announced an expenditure of $225,000 for the yards, round-house and shops at Smithers. Foley, Welch and Stewart received a big contract for building the huge ditches to drain the swamp at Smithers.

Even with the warmer weather the roads, in some sections, never dried out. The government road between Barrett's Diamond D Ranch and the McInnes Ranch was in a terrible state. Freighters said it was the worst they had ever seen. Superintendent J.C. Sheppard and Duncan Ross had the misfortune of travelling through and said three four-horse teams were on a load of a single ton and still could not move it. Through that one section, a travelling rate of three miles (about five kilometres) a day was the expected maximum. George T. Wall travelled from Fort George to New Hazelton and saw the worst roads imaginable between Aldermere and Decker Lake. He described poor horses wallowing in the mud, wagons stuck to the tops of their wheels, mud up to wagon boxes. Fortunately for Wall he was riding a single horse and was able to pick his way around the mud pits to Aldermere by riding most of the time in the bush.

The early auto stages ran over these very challenging road conditions. W.J. "Wiggs" O'Neill's Russell-Knight car and Packard truck operated between New Hazelton and Aldermere. He also advertised an auto stage between Aldermere and over Bulkley Summit to Duncan Ross's camp near Rose Lake. In June 1913, William W. Wrathall took his "Indian motorcycle" on a fast trip from New Hazelton to Decker Lake and back, zipping around all the mudholes. An insurance salesman from Vancouver also travelled the grade by motorcycle selling insurance to anyone who would buy it. After reading about the GTP construction and no doubt some of its fatalities, an undertaker from Vancouver toured the region and considered the possibility of opening a business in New Hazelton. A special trip was made by the Anglican bishop of Caledonia, Bishop Frederick Herbert DuVernet of Prince Rupert. The bishop travelled by train to the end of steel and walked on to the camps for a personal look at the men and the camp conditions.

In the summer of 1913, Bill Jasper made an epic trip supplying fresh beef to camps for Pat Burns and Company. He was the first to come through on a wagon from Fort George to Hazelton and considering the poor conditions of the road this was a major

The homestead on Charlie Barrett's Diamond D Ranch. *Bulkley Valley Museum, P1350*

feat. Jasper travelled overland from Kamloops with three hundred head of cattle. The animals were ferried across the Nechako River and taken across Burns and Decker lakes by scows. One hundred were left at camps at Burns Lake and a similar number at Decker Lake. Jasper drove the remaining cattle to an abattoir on Mission Point near Hazelton; the meat supplied the local market the rest of the summer and fall.

The pioneer farmers who had painstakingly cleared land and established crops and livestock earned their rewards when they slaughtered some of their cattle for camps and sold their hay for top dollar. The railway camps proved to be a guaranteed market and farmers sold out of every shipment of their freshly dug potatoes at six cents a pound. Established farmers expanded; Archie McInnes shipped in a carload of cattle to add to his stock at his McInnes Ranch and a carload of laying hens was brought in for a farm near New Hazelton. Farmers tried new crops and found success; A. Blayney of Ootsa Lake planted three acres of Red Fife wheat and farmers at Chicken Lake had great results with Marquis wheat, Maudsbury barley and Red Fife wheat. The early crops at the end of summer were heavy; hay yielded two tons to the acre. Barrett's

Diamond D Ranch put up three hundred tons of hay and six hundred tons of potatoes that year.

The summer of 1913 also brought welcome news to the miners. The GTP announced a $2 a ton reduction on the rate of freight. Mines shipped out the large stockpiles of ore and brought in larger gangs to work their claims. Silver Standard Mines shipped three hundred tons of ore out of New Hazelton in ten carloads. Residents came out to see the train off and waved to the decorated cars. Crowds all along the line came out and watched it pass by because they believed it was the richest freight shipped on the GTP line so far. They were right. The returns from the Trail Smelter were $30,000.61 or $106.42 per ton. Mine exports picked up; the first shipment of coal from the Grand Trunk BC Coal Property left New Hazelton bound for Nanaimo's Gas and Coke Company Works. Harris Mines sent out a carload that went for over $70 a ton and the Erie Mine sent a carload that sold for over $100 a ton.

The high returns on farms and mines spilled over into the coastal fishery. Fish-

The townsite of Smithers before the tracks were laid, June 1913. *Bulkley Valley Museum, P2598*

The tracklayer reaches the Telkwa River and a large crowd of locals from Telkwa, Hubert and Aldermere come to watch the noisy machine and hard-working men. *Bulkley Valley Museum, P1079*

ing out of Prince Rupert was big business. During the month of August half a million dollars worth of fish was handled in the port. The salmon weighed a total of 8.4 million pounds (3.8 million kilograms) and there were one million pounds of halibut caught.

Through the intense efforts of the contractors and the unflagging hard work of the labourers, the cutting and filling of the rail grade advanced. D.A. Rankin's contract, where Leslie worked, was in the thick of cutting out hundreds of tons of excess earth and creating a level grade. Near to Leslie and Bernice, John Bostrom completed one contract and moved his steam shovel and men to a huge 250,000 cubic yard fill across the Nechako River at Fort Fraser. Rankin's Wharf at Decker Lake moved an average of fifteen tons a day to the Burns Lake freight depot. Johnny Albi finished his contract near Decker Lake and arrived in New Hazelton thin and worn out, on his way to visit relatives in Spokane for a brief rest. He admitted to driving a grading team of horses himself in order to stay well ahead of the tracklayer.

John W. Stewart of Foley, Welch and Stewart announced that the GTP track-laying team from the eastern leg of construction would reach Fort George in the winter of 1913 and estimated the track-laying team working its way west through the Bulkley Valley should pass Barrett Ranch, McInnes Ranch, Rose Lake and Decker Lake to reach Burns Lake by the winter of 1913. John W. Stewart guessed the line would be completed in the spring of 1914. He noted that all camps were going full force and urging men, machinery and horses to the maximum extent.

With so much activity and so many men employed near Decker Lake and Burns Lake, two constables moved to Decker Lake and attempted to keep peace throughout the camps and tried to shut down the blind pigs.

⌒

Home Sweet Home, Decker Lake
Tuesday Evening
June 3, 1913

My dearest family,

Well, we did stay over the extra day at Barrett's then left about 1:30 Friday afternoon for home and drove to Mr. Robey's for the night. Skookum Johnson, resident engineer, welcomed us with a hearty "walk right in" and we and our four kittens settled about the camp as though we owned it.

I walked most of the distance for Leslie did not care to report throwing me and there was no way around the mud holes. He had to drive right through. The wheels of the carriage would stand at the sharpest angle with Leslie hanging on with one hand and driving with the other. How the rig stood it I do not see.

We left Robey's, Johnson's Camp, and drove three quarters of a mile to the Albis Camp.

Right at their front door lay a mud hole. No turn about so Les drove in up to the hubs and had the horses on hard bottom. They were doing nicely until Jack got into a soft hole and went down. Poor horse tried three times to get up then dropped. I got out by jumping from the wheel and went up to the camp. The men grinned and started out at once. Les had unhooked the team and Molly had pulled Jack out. A big freight team came up and hitched their leaders onto the pole of our rig. With a man prying the hub up with a log the buggy got out.

Charlie Barrett expanded operations on his Diamond D Ranch to take advantage of the railway camps' need for food for the men and feed for the horses. *Bulkley Valley Museum, P1354*

We got on without further accident and we reached Duncan Ross's camp. Met the new line doctor, Mr. Kearney returning from Ross's camp where he had been to look Stanley McNaughton over after his horse rolled on him in a mud hole.

Then we were almost up to Danses Roadhouse when a hole just before a high stump let us down so that the stump struck instead of allowing the buggy to go over. Crash, jar, splinter and the double tree was twins. Leslie said "Oh hell you, Jack, and now the double tree. I wonder what next."

But that made the trio of accidents. I held the horses while Leslie spliced [the double tree] with its own holdback strap and most of the rope which was holding the kittens' box onto the back of the rig. We did reach home with no other serious accident.

At the Danses Roadhouse the Bulkley River makes a roaring foaming drop of 20 feet. Lots of water through a tremendous current.

Over the hill, through a long poplar grove, dodging mud holes and crossing lots of short pieces of corduroy, out onto the grade where we could speed up. If the road is passable we are not allowed on the grade. Then around the edge of a marsh, up

Freighters rushed through the rail camps along the construction route of the Grand Trunk Pacific Railway. *The Fraser Fort George Museum Society and the Exploration Place, P985-51-4*

over the grade again and into a mile of lodge pole pine. Here we met the faithful Edward with the swing. He reported only eight mud holes between Snyder's Roadhouse and Decker Lake.

Next past a curve of river where Pat Burns is watering 35 big beef cattle en route to the camp meat houses. Up and down and then a lovely little lake, perhaps a mile in length. Over stumps, or through mud all the same, swim, plow.

Through Captain McLeod's camp and up a long hill where Edward had to use a twelve-horse team to pull a four-horse load two days before. Down a hill where the horses had to sit and slide and through a ford where the water, up to the side of the box of the buggy, swirled some of the mud off. Past a ranch where the proprietor was carefully tending a fire guard at the edge of his property.

The horses began to speed up despite the mud and ruts for we were nearing Snyder's Roadhouse. Fresh beef steak, good tea and potatoes (after six meals of ham, bacon, boiled tea and no potatoes) and we started for the last lap. Those eight mud holes Edward reported were actually fourteen mud holes and then half a mile of corduroy (6 inch cottonwood logs) to the entry of Decker Lake.

The cabin looks so nice. The ground is all cleared and the brush is off between us and the lake. The garden is started and the Peterborough canoe is a pippin.
Goodnight sweetness and a bushel of love,
Bernice

DECKER LAKE
JUNE 30, 1913

My dearest Mother,

Oh you, miles and miles. I am glad I am here but the cheerful part is that we will be done here by December 1st. The steel will be here to take us out. Mr. Tuck was here and seemed very cheerful so I think we may be too, for he is the greatest pessimist in the crowd. The next trip I take will be on the GTP, rah, rah.

Mr. D.A. Rankin himself was up here. He took the 24 miles of PGE near Lillooet and is having one large time of it I guess. No men to be had, poor roads, no supplies etc. Our food supply is alright and, as far as we are personally concerned, we are very comfortable. The business just now is keeping the men guessing.

The laborers camp out. They are independent of a job.

This rain is keeping the cost of freighting way up. One storekeeper here just paid 12 cents a pound on a load of freight.

I can't imagine a lovelier place to spend the summer. We walk, paddle or swim, the water is fine. We use our mosquito tent over our bed when they happen to be bad.

Founder of Terrace BC
George Little, 1878-1955

In the summer of 1913 George Little, the owner of the Terrace townsite and the Terrace lumber mills, came upriver to Hazelton to promote his settlement. The new community of Terrace was starting to expand and Little boasted there were buildings going up, fruit trees being planted, a ballpark being built and a tennis court constructed. He hoped Terrace would become the agricultural centre of the North and invited interior residents to tour his town. If the greenhouses, fruit trees and parks weren't enough for a prospective settler, Little had somehow managed to cobble together an impressive twenty-five-piece brass band.

Photo: Yvonne Moen, personal collection

The tracklayer near Telkwa, summer 1913. *Telkwa Museum, P0148*

I have a garden. My vegetables are fair. With half a chance at sunshine they would be fine. I had two little flowerbeds but the swing was here the other day and the two horses put to grass and most of the elephants came to the flowerbeds. If the flowers don't grow I can go out and find some in the woods. I found some lovely wild sweet peas, yellow shirt stem daisies, white violets.

This morning I had the pip with unusual vigour. Due no doubt to the shaking up I got on that ride for I was sick then too. It gave me a long lazy day and I am feeling fine now.

Tell Marj that if she wants a fellow I'll catch her one. Even the great, fat Sheppard asked, "Well, when is sister coming?" You see we have just had a romance here with a capital R. Mrs. Kerr's friend, Mamie Blanchard, was planning to go back to marry a man she was not crazy about. So when she had been gone ten days and Dan Stenstrom, the head clerk under Mr. Smith, asked ten days vacation to bring Mamie back there was some excitement. You see he handles all the business work with the various

contractors and the GTP. So everyone was interested. We raised a purse of over $1000 and bought a chest of flat silver, a tea set, all house and bed linen. I think this affair has awakened all the unmarried men. Besides the gifts, the GTP gave them a pass for all the branch lines and the coast boats to Vancouver until the RR is finished.
Bushels of love,
Bernice

DECKER LAKE, BC
JULY 1, 1913

My dear Ruth,
This is the Canadian anniversary of the joining of the various provinces into a unit and is kept as we keep our fourth of July.

Many of the hanger-ons about town have gone to the end of the lake for the day for a little celebration. Yesterday the GTP engineers, from headquarters five miles above here, had a boat go the length of the two lakes and gather the men from the residencies on the way.

Since I came home I have been very busy. I walked into an iron rod and disfigured my nose for ten days. I've washed everything in sight including blankets, curtains and the family heads. Have now retired from washing in favor of "Sing Lee, Laundry, Baths, Bread," he will do all "washa" at ten dollars a month.

Our canoe is a pippin and after our supper we often paddle out into the middle of the lake with our books and sewing for the sunset hour. I can't make Les read aloud, he is the worst mule about some things.

My garden is growing fast. We will have lettuce in a week and that will be a godsend. I bought fruit when I was in Rupert and am ordering again now. Shipped to end of steel c/o FW&S where our swing picks them up.

It has rained so much I fear our roads will never dry.

Don't know when it will be but as we ought to finish here in November or December and, as there is no Baby Martin in prospect, I think I may get there before many months.

Had Lee Sing, or "Willie" as the men call him, here yesterday to wash and bake, as I was sick with the pip.

Six pm and I have the letters to post and supper to get.

The wind howls so think we can't go out in the canoe tonight.

Bushels of love to you both,

Bernice MM

DECKER LAKE
TUESDAY, JULY 8, 1913

My dearest Father,

It has become regular to have rain and the rare thing to have sunshine. The roads are beyond even a hardened skinner's vocabulary to express.

A big tunnel near New Hazelton has caved in. It will be a week before the way is clear. That tunnel is through gumbo and had not yet been concreted. End of steel has crossed Trout Creek at Moricetown and is now moving toward Aldermere with no obstacle or bridge in its way.

I guess Mr. Dempsey's boast of Aldermere by July 28 is probably safe, unless they send him back to fix the tunnel or if some of his supplies are on the other side of the tunnel. When they get to Aldermere they will encounter the Bulkley and the Telkwa rivers. Just one long, low bridge and then on to Decker Lake.

There is lots of unfinished grade this side of Aldermere and we are told that steel may not reach us by Christmas.

Duncan Cameron was here last night for a call. He is foreman for Duncan Ross on the work near Ehlrich's where I stayed last summer. He brought a girl in from Aldermere, who was going to work at Frances Lake on a confinement case. She came from Victoria. What some of these English girls do is beyond me. Now she was coming on the various stages and the roads got so bad no man who can help it is traveling. The FW&S swings are all held up. Few independent freighters or gippos (gypsies by the road as they come to save money) are working at 12 ½ cents a pound. When the girl reached Aldermere she was advised to "get that man over there," Duncan Cameron, to take her out. And when she asked he said yes though it is sixty miles more journey than he would have had to drive. From there she goes by boat. Some trip I guess.

Last year the autos ran all summer from the 16th of June on from Hazelton to Aldermere. Not one trip this year.

Today I ironed and a call on a sick neighbor then came back to get a little dinner for two. When Leslie came in the door he shouted, "One more plate, Mrs. Martin."

I looked around the corner and saw Mr. Warks, one of the Prince Rupert jewellers. He was almost sick with his trip but said he had to keep on the road for there was no money circulating among the retail men in Prince Rupert. He said that the building of Prince Rupert is going right along. Everyone talks Fort George now. It will be the same story as it has been with Prince Rupert and Vancouver. The man who gets in early with a little capital can turn it over two or three times in the early days and make big profits.

I do wonder what our next

Visiting officials, four miles (six kilometres) from Moricetown. Left to right: Sir Alfred Waldron Smithers, Lady Doughty and Sir Doughty. *Bulkley Valley Museum, P0689*

move will be. Les says he has no idea. He hopes to have a month's vacation in Seattle before he starts anything new. A mine railroad I expect. Maybe the Pacific Great Eastern from Fort George to Vancouver. We have been very happy and comfortable so far and I don't seem to worry about the future.

In a couple of weeks we expect semi-weekly mail service. Oh, we are prospering, I can tell you. Decker Lake is quite a burg. We have no more blind pigs for we have a very efficient police force, Mr. McGin and Mr. Munroe. Mr. Monroe is fond of sailing and is on the lake most of the time. The other day a good husky storm blew up and I watched the boat. She flew by like a bird and I wondered who the other guy was with Munroe. When I went to the offices and found the door locked I soon found out. Les said that the wind was too good to pass up.

Now Pap we still hope to be out of here in December, will you and the family meet us in Seattle or Tacoma for a month?

Let me hear from you before too long,

Bushels of love to all the family,

Bernice

DECKER LAKE, BC
MONDAY, JULY 21, 1913

My dear Ruth,

Summer has come at last. Five successive hot days. We like it for it is such a change. True it breeds mosquitoes and black flies but we fight those off.

I had Honest John fix a little framework over the bed to make the mosquito canopy higher. He is a slow moving German who takes all day for a little job and spends half the time going back to the warehouse for a tool. In the morning he and I made an icebox. A 5 gallon oil can opened on its long side, set into a powder box and packed with paper and moss, and for a cover a piece of cheesecloth. That makes better ventilation and the tiny box keeps the butter, food etc. cold.

Last night the tug Conveyor went down five miles to Stewart's Camp and I was invited to ride from 7 to 9:30 in the light of the loveliest sunset.

This is not a place of stagnation. Les came in to demand a list of groceries which we want to order from the wholesale house. Mrs. Bailey followed him, then Mrs. Ross. I was not cleaned up. I dressed and sat down to write when bang bang bang. I thought a load of powder must be going up and raced out to the lake to look and realized it was only stumps going up.

Bushels of love,

Bernice

The Death of John "Broken Nose Kelly"

Surprisingly Bernice did write home to her mother about the shooting of "Broken Nose Kelly." Here is the whole story:

On a summer evening in early August 1913, at Burns Lake, Jerry Mulvilhill encountered his old acquaintance John Kelly, a.k.a. "Denver Ed" or "Broken Nose Kelly." For the last two years Denver Ed had worked at various camps along the line, including the Skeena Crossing Bridge and in the summer of 1913 was employed at Decker Lake. The two men had an altercation and Jerry Mulvilhill left to locate a gun. In the wee hours of the morning an angry Jerry Mulvilhill saw Denver Ed inside a building, thrust a rifle through a window and fired. The bullet passed through Denver Ed's head and caused his death two hours later.

Constables McGin and Munro were summoned from Decker Lake and arrested Mulvilhill. Chief Gam-mon was summoned from New Hazelton.

Days later the Deputy Coroner Wallace and Constable MacAulay arrived and held an inquest. The prisoner was escorted to Aldermere's jail where he received his preliminary trial on the charge of murder.

Mulvilhill was found guilty of murder and sentenced to hang December 29, 1913.

DECKER LAKE, BC
JULY 29, 1913

Dearest Marjorie,

I just put on my shoes thinking I would walk to the office and see if the mail was in when the most awful downpour of rain commences. I have a good fire in the heater though the windows in the room are open.

Cheer up and think of the joys of life. 1: this is mail day. 2: I have eight letters ready to go out. 3: saw a family of grouse the day before. 4: Mr. Barrett sent a great bundle of rhubarb. 5: Les is growing fat. 6: Had a ride on the *Conveyor* the other day. 7: Borrowed Mrs. B's sewing machine and finished two crepe combinations. 8: Went swimming with Les, Harris, Alma and Bob (a black fly bit my eye). 9: the Chinese are bidding against each other for my washing. 10: I had a party and it went off splendidly. 11: Almost through with the pip without any complications this time so I congratulate myself. There, that is certainly a list of cheers.

Les just came over to say that the mail was not in and would I like to have Mr. Sprauge come to supper as he brought the rhubarb. I must say yes and get up and cook something. No fresh meat for ten days and I have a brain fog over the what to eat question.

Here I go to the kitchen.
Bushels of love,
Bernice

DECKER LAKE, BC
JULY 31, 1913

My dearie Mother,

Yesterday a box of meat and bread came up from camp. The first beef in twelve days. This time it was four little steaks, a piece of tenderloin and a big roast.

By good fortune we had it yesterday when Mr. Sprauge came to dinner. He is so charming and so hated by the contractors in his capacity as an engineer. He is one of those men whose conscience works overtime and who pinches the contractor at every turn. You see the contract says approximately so many yards are to be cut out and so many filled in. Now that is classified as "rock," "gravel," "earth" and the engineer in residence, and his assistant, classify and measure. Suppose it was gumbo, that is mud, naturally it would be of "earth." Now if the season was so dry that it had to be blasted

Smithers BC June 1913

The temporary shelters and shacks of the newly created town of Smithers. *Bulkley Valley Museum, P0214*

out and moved in chunks that work would cost the contractors as much as if it were "solid rock." Most engineers would classify it so. But the book says gumbo is "earth," so "earth" it is to Sprauge and his men. Leslie has often said he did wish Sprauge was in any work but ours.

There are three things that have stirred up railroad circles in these woods lately:

1. The Spokane papers reporting the arrest and trial of Mrs. C. Van———for pandering, wife of the head of the engineer on the western division of the GTP.

2. The shooting of a man through the window of a poolroom at the little town on the other end of Burns Lake. A quarrel earlier in the evening over a poker game, the threat, "I'll get you in the morning," the knowledge of a four year old grudge of Klondike days, all tend to point to one man as the murderer. But there is no proof at all. Coroner's jury are holding trial and making no headway at all. The man shot was "Broken Nose Kelly," a professional gambler.

3. The fact that officials and B.B. Kelliher are at last coming through. The party came up from Vancouver when I did in the spring but they turned back because the roads were so bad.

The track-laying boss, Dan Dempsey, overseeing the laying of track near Telkwa. *Bulkley Valley Museum, P0187*

Oh, in the evening we had such fun. Les and I were going sailing and in came the local blacksmith, Gus Dahr, half-baked, bareheaded, dirty faced with corduroy trousers half up under his arms held there by suspenders, while the fullness was held in by a belt at the waistline. Well Gus talked and upon a little tactful questioning he was bound across the lake to see something he had there. With his hints and talk one would have thought it was a gold mine but a husbandly wink made me expect a whiskey cache. We never made the shore for the wind died down so we barely crawled home under the sail. It was such fun. Gus talked of jumping claims, of figures in the clouds, of people staying in little dead towns waiting for a bonanza until they went crazy and about Tony the dog's prowess as a swimmer.

In another month I shall be going out gun in hand every day, for the season for grouse will open and we will be glad for a change in diet. I have a new reel and line for our old pole and it does very well.

A bushel of love to you,

Bernice MM

FALL 1913

"Two days ago the steel had not yet reached Fort George from the other end yet and all the way to here the grade is in process of construction and patches were finished every little way."

Captain McLeod's camp. *Telkwa Museum, P0147*

Bernice and Leslie, like all the other residents in the North in the autumn of 1913, were excited by the progress of the rails. Completion seemed closer to a reality when the passenger service was first extended to the temporary station at Smithers and then on to the temporary depot at Telkwa. On October 11 the first passenger train arrived in Smithers from Prince Rupert filled with many coastal residents who came to the Bulkley Valley to sightsee and to escape the rains. The tracks were laid east from Telkwa, along the (west side of the) Bulkley River, past Barrett Ranch at South Bulkley and past McInnes Ranch at North Bulkley and towards Rose Lake. But only the work trains lumbered east out of Telkwa. The tracklayer waited at Paget's contract for a huge fill to be finished.

While the tracklayer waited for the grade to be levelled, the fall rains caused creeks to burst their banks and portions of the rail grade along the Skeena were once again washed out. Slides occurred at Hardscrabble and Fiddler Creek. Dan Dempsey and his large crew of men were brought in from end of steel to repair the slides and they worked all night to repair the crossing over Fiddler Creek and at daybreak marched westward to repair the slide at Hardscrabble Creek. In the fall of 1913 labourers all along the line welcomed the arrival of the ditcher, a long-promised piece of equipment.

There were injuries associated with pushing workers late into the night. A man walking on the tracks at night was run over by a speeder. A night brakeman fell under a car and one arm and one leg were crushed. A night labourer in a tunnel was badly injured when a lantern fell from the roof of the tunnel, struck him on the head and exploded. Dr. Wrinch in Hazelton welcomed the assistance of another doctor nearby, Dr. Wallace in Telkwa. After an inspection

The long-awaited ditcher arrives for the final leg of construction between Decker and Fraser lakes. *Northern BC Archives and Special Collections, Prince George Railway and Forestry Museum Society, PGE Harlow Collection, 2002.1.30.4.94*

of the railway camps east of Telkwa, Dr. Wallace notified the public of an outbreak of diphtheria among the men and advised everyone to be very careful.

As the grade was levelled and readied for Dan Dempsey and his tracklayer, worn-out contractors and labourers left the area. Duncan Ross finished his contract and went home to Victoria for a rest. An exhausted Superintendent J. Sheppard was struck down with inflammatory rheumatism at Barrett Ranch and was sent to Prince Rupert for recovery.

The effusive J.W. Stewart of Foley, Welch and Stewart continued to praise the natural resources of the northern part of British Columbia and said he strongly believed that with the completion of the GTPR the next spring the wealth of the district would be realized. He referred to the Pacific Great Eastern rails coming to Prince George and speculated on a rail line running north from Hazelton over the mountains to

The Smithers railway yards and freshly laid multiple tracks, October 1913. *Bulkley Valley Museum, P2596*

Alaska. Even Sir Richard McBride believed in the GTPR and the positive role it was sure to have on the northern region. He claimed that the GTP would increase immigration to the North, create large cities, generate jobs and allow the export of the area's agricultural and mineral wealth.

In 1913 the Wakefields, pioneer ranchers since 1907, took advantage of the freight cars coming to Telkwa and imported a shipment of breeding stock for their dairy farm east of Telkwa. The temporary depot facility at Telkwa was extremely busy; there were twenty-one carloads of merchandise, settlers' effects and farm produce shipped in from Prince Rupert. Bulkley Valley farmers had had a great summer; within a twenty-mile (thirty-two-kilometre) radius of Telkwa twenty-five hundred tons of hay was put up. Leslie no doubt would have ordered shipments of area produce for D.A. Rankin's camp. The farms supplied many of the work camps near Rose, Decker and Burns lakes moving their produce, potatoes and hay on the work trains headed east, up the line out of Telkwa, on an average of four railcar loads a day. Hay was sold at $30 a ton on the car.

The New Hazelton Mine Owners Association formed. The men sent a large display of ore to the Prince Rupert Fall Fair, which resulted in a clean sweep. The gold commissioner and government agent in New Hazelton, Stephen Hoskins, rallied optimism after he inspected the mines in the district. Some mines stopped work when winter approached but others felt the excitement of high ore returns and chose to drive cross tunnels all winter long.

The snow arrived in the mountains and would soon cover the northern towns. A record number of passengers showed up to catch the train out of New Hazelton before winter weather descended. It was standing-room-only on the two coaches heading to Prince Rupert. Many labourers, miners and businessmen returned to warmer climates for the winter. Many railroaders left camp and returned home to their families, some planning to return in the spring.

Sheady and Smith moved their headquarters from Bulkley Summitt near Barrett's ranch farther inland to Stella at Fraser Lake. Foley, Welch and Stewart built some large barns to accommodate the many workhorses at freighting headquarters at Decker Lake. In the fall of 1913 Leslie Martin was tracking the hours of five hundred to one thousand men working at Burns and Decker lakes. Stewart Brothers and D.A. Rankin rushed to complete their work. The railway commissioner announced that Mile 301 near Decker Lake would be the winter terminus but tried to reduce the risk of incidents by enforcing a six-mile-an-hour limit over any and all bridges.

〜

Mrs. L.F. Martin's Butter Factory
September 1913, Decker Lake, BC
Wednesday morning, dark and dripping.
Weather forecast, gol-darned.
Money market, squashed flat.

My dear Daddy,

This week has been very busy. I had a man working with me in the house, trying to renovate some butter for Leslie. Earlier in the summer I complained of the butter Les had in the warehouse and later the camps complained of it. After a while he got at it

The interior of the Smithers roundhouse. *Bulkley Valley Museum, P1364*

and opened it up, some 400 pounds. It was mouldy, not rancid. Had not been well washed at the factory nor salted enough. Les put all the good in their thin foil paper wrappings into casks of brine and the really bad he was going to dump. He said if I could fix six boxes, 300 pounds, he would give me fifty dollars. I melted, boiled, skimmed, strained, cooled, washed in chloride of lime water and then in clear water, salted. Not fit yet. We took it in easy stages but it was messy and took three days to do 100 pounds. We are going to use the rest for fuel I guess, or sell it to the Chinaman for washing out clothes.

—

For days it has rained nearly all day and the roads are beginning to cut up. That does not affect heavy freighting for the end of steel is only about ten miles from here and the freight camp is moving to that point now…The road is being ballasted and will be rushed until snow or frost overtakes the work.

Two days ago the steel had not yet reached Fort George from the other end yet and all the way to here the grade is in process of construction and patches were finished every little way.

Mr. Sands's Auto Trip

September 1913 brought an unlikely sight to the rutted wagon roads of northern BC: an "auto touring car" driven by Mr. Sands and carrying three other passengers. Identified passengers were Alexander Powell and Mr. Kuhn. Bernice did not write home about it but no doubt she must have heard about the car as it struggled past Decker Lake.

The men had travelled from Mexico to Hazelton. The *Interior News* of Aldermere stated it was the first auto to make the trip. "The cyclometer of the machine showed that a distance of three thousand miles was covered between San Francisco to Aldermere" wrote Joseph Coyle, editor of the *Interior News*.

The roads were heavily used horse and wagon freight trails and the auto had to be portaged over a few miles of unfinished roads and around the occasional mudhole.

Near Telkwa the touring men met up with GTP General Superintendent Meehan and his private railcar and asked Meehan if a flatcar and some labourers could be provided to them once they reached the depot at New Hazelton. The travellers wanted their auto put on a railcar to Prince Rupert. Meehan, likely feeling the pressure of the coming winter and the inevitable trials of the construction, was gruff in his rebuke to the tourists.

The car bumped its way to New Hazelton and was loaded onto a railcar with no help from the officials of the GTP. After arriving in Prince Rupert the car and men took a steamer to Vancouver and Victoria and toured Vancouver Island. The tourists took the time to write a scathing letter to the area papers about Meehan's lack of hospitality.

The construction of Foley, Welch and Stewart's large storage cache at Decker Lake. *Bulkley Valley Museum, P0530*

Les feels safe that his work won't hold up the steel at all so his reputation as a contractor is safe though he won't make much money I fear.

The new official government approved townsite of Fort George goes onto the marker in Vancouver today. Lots are sold at auction to the highest bidder. Quarter price of lot to be paid down, balance in 1, 2, and 3 years.

Les thinks we better stay on here while he gets the work in shape and use the 42 horses freighting from the lower end of Burns Lake east to the contractors who are working in there for the last lap of this Grand Trunk Pacific.

If Foley, Welch and Stewart maintain their big cache here all winter then freighting will be down the lake on the ice.

You see we make the cost of the outfit first (the four kitchen outfits, dump cars, one steam shovel, stock, four donkey engines, rails), second the salaries for Tuck, H. Rankin and Les, then third D.A. Rankin's percentage and fourth is profit.

If there is no profit due to unexpected delay in advance of steel and consequent cost of freight, we will have the outfit and our $150 a month salary so we are not exactly in the poor house.

If the work runs too low the Foley, Welch and Stewart men will ask the engineering staff to raise the estimates, i.e. make loose rock out of earth on the books. That is a detail of the technical recording I am not up on.

—

Us and the Bowness' bought a cow. Her calf drank all the milk. The calf was made veal. The cow ran away. It cost $4 to get her back. We tied her out to pasture. Someone milked her and let her go. We got her back. She gives ten quarts of milk a day.

Soon she will be roast beef. Poor cow.

Don't tell everyone all you read in my letters.

I love you all ten bushels and a half,

Bernice

Dearest Marjorie,

Mail day and your darling contributions and packages from Simpson's. Shirts, pajamas, hat, safety pins, ribbon, hairpins etc.

This is a perfect day. Alma, Mrs. Ross and I are going into the woods after high-bush cranberries. Little transparent red fellows that make a beautiful jelly.

Say Marj, the accommodation passenger train is coming within 9 miles of us on October 5th, rah rah—$20 Seattle to Prince Rupert inclusive of berth and meals. Come on up won't you and mama?

Seems I am never ready for the mail.

Your sister,

Bernice

DECKER LAKE
OCTOBER 6, 1913

Dearest Mother,

Last night we had some of this season's ducks. We did enjoy it. All of us had some including our animals.

Yes, we have our fire going. Have had it almost all summer, a bit in the morning and late at night.

Main Street, Smithers. *Bulkley Valley Museum, P1308*

Grand Trunk Pacific train transferring freight onto horse-drawn sleds for hauling to camps beyond Rose Lake. *Bulkley Valley Museum, P0733*

Now it never quite goes out. Those airtight heaters are great fun. Fire starts in one minute and keeps for ten or twelve hours when the stove is shut off.

Yesterday we had a cold rain with the least bit of a snow flurry. Today is gorgeous. Frost bright on the ground and sun bright overhead.

The mixed train is coming to Bulkley Summit twice a week from now on. Until the road is ballasted for the regular passenger run and that is only nine miles from here. Back of the house for two miles either way the grade is in construction—wheelbarrow work with men digging the dirt at the side and piling it in the middle to make the grade.

Here I find a little paper with a note I made last January on the cost of our work.

Month of January, 1913

Camp 1: Cost $15,680.18

Camp 2: Cost $4,571.98

Camp 3: Cost $10,243.34

This is exclusive of freight paid out by D.A. Rankin Company to Foley, Welch and Stewart for moving the steam shovel and donkey engines. Shovel freight is $6,500 and for two donkeys $1,700. That was during the winter when the freight rates were high and everything was expensive. But it was a very average month. It shows the enormous cost of this work.

Just now Les has greatest pleasure in the fact that the boat is doing well. She cost some $1,200 and the man who runs her draws $100 per month. But she has paid for herself and running on one cylinder, as she did this month, cleared $700. Les is doing all the D.A. Rankin freight.

Three other subcontractors freighting, a few outsiders (ranchers, storekeepers) and now the company has had to come to Les to help out.

The big Foley, Welch and Stewart superintendent of construction, Mr. Sheppard, was stricken with inflammatory rheumatism and had to be taken out on stretcher. He is recovering rapidly but has gone to a hot spring in Missouri. He left behind a young cub he was training to run his errands. Shep himself had admitted he had picked a poor stick and was looking for a better one but he was taken so suddenly. Now the cub is in trouble all the time, does everything he ought not to, gives orders to everyone and is a general goat. He will get canned soon we expect. Little things like that are the local gossip and keep us all chattering.

I hear the horses kicking in the barn. It reminds me that so many horses have swamp fever. One died in our barn last night. Not ours, praise be, though we have lost three horses at camp.

Hope to have the Parkers from Prince Rupert out for Christmas. Mr. Parker has a new business proposition on foot. To buy another small outfit if they can arrange it right, which will make them one or two fair-sized outfits. Then if they could only buy a passenger bus next year and let Mr. Parker run it. And same as now, we all go railroading. We could be something ahead one day.

I feel as though we are not doing very badly.

We are going to order oysters, sausage, Christmas lilies, and celery this order. Goodbye, my love to all the family,

Your little Bernice

WINTER 1913-14

"The real cold is coming now after the thaw and the lake is booming as it freezes. It is a sheet of glass and I am going to borrow skates and turn out with the crowd tonight."

The tracklayer moved down the snow-packed right-of-way and neared the point of completion. *Bulkley Valley Museum, P0250*

The winter of 1913 was a very busy one for the few police stationed in rustic quarters in Hazelton, Aldermere and Decker Lake. A fight at a canvas cookhouse in Decker Lake resulted in two men being badly injured when another man attacked them with an axe. A squabble at a GTP camp near Rose Lake over dwindling food supplies turned ugly when a rifle was shot through a closed cabin door, injuring labourer Alfred Wright. The shooter was brought to the jail in New Hazelton. There was a drunken fight and murder in Telkwa. There was even a bank robbery in New Hazelton. Faced with lawlessness the police force cracked down where they could—they focused on the offences of operating a blind pig and carrying a concealed weapon.

One freighter was charged with providing liquor without a licence and was promptly sentenced to six months in jail at New Westminster. Another man had an especially unlucky day when a barrel bounced off his wagon near Decker Lake and broke open. The constable riding a horse behind him stopped to help him out with his cargo and then arrested him for transporting a wagonload of whiskey. The man had five barrels on the wagon, each containing 560 bottles of whiskey. He was sentenced to twelve months in jail.

Police in Aldermere, Telkwa and New Hazelton made arrests or issued fines for carrying concealed weapons. A man was arrested in Smithers for carrying a pistol concealed in his pant leg. One labourer was found carrying a knife with a seven-inch blade under his overcoat. Despite his claim that it was only used to clean his shoes, Magistrate Hoskins charged him $15.

Tensions ran high and tragedy resulted. A fast-walking, pocket-clutching man was followed through the bush near Skeena Crossing by Special Constable Quinlivin and a tracker named Magnus Edgar. The constable and the tracker thought the man was one of the escaped bank robbers. Tracker Edgar fired shots that were meant to stop him but unfortunately fatally wounded the man. The dead man turned out to be a long-time labourer employed by Foley, Welch and Stewart, clutching his pocket full of cashed time cheques and rushing to return to camp. To add to the tragedy the tracker Magnus Edgar was charged with murder.

Despite the "Wild West" behaviour erupting in camps and northern towns the Grand Trunk Pacific advanced. In the beginning of winter the work and freight trains reached close to Decker Lake and the local merchants had a moment of perhaps foolish optimism. They ordered several boxes of fish from Prince Rupert. Of course the train with the fish was delayed departing and when it reached Rose Lake it could not get past a frost heave in the tracks. The men at Rose Lake Camp said the freight cars smelled pretty bad and that the boxes of fish would soon walk up to Decker Lake by themselves.

Delays were common and residents came to expect at least a twelve-hour wait. Locals assumed that the train would arrive and leave late and more than one resident was surprised to see the caboose of their passenger train making a rare on-time departure.

Mud Creek crossing gave labourers and engineers a lot of trouble. First slides came down near the bridge and then three hundred feet (ninety-one metres) of fill east of Mud Creek disappeared in a sinkhole. After much head-scratching and many hours of shovelling, the GTP engineers agreed to widen the cuts at Mud Creek by several

Knowing the track-laying gang is gaining on them, the men work hard on clearing a big cut near Burns Lake. *Bulkley Valley Museum, P0495*

hundred feet where the slides had reoccurred. Rock men were brought in to blast the material down for the steam shovel to lift out.

Large slides occurred at Mile 125; trees and rocks were carried down and created a huge pile several feet high beyond the local section crew. The FWS derrick and crew went down but they too were stymied. When all else failed they sent for Dan Dempsey's large crew of labourers who came and shovelled the slide debris off the track.

There were more washouts and more slides. A mudslide at the Kitselas tunnels covered one end of the tracks. One freight train barrelled right through it but the next one became stuck.

The GTP were criticized for their two-tenths grade. Most agreed that insisting on a "prairie grade" through difficult terrain was the cause of the trouble but also admitted that the landslides and washouts of the winter of 1913 employed more men and created good business. The GTP, the subcontractors and many of the men holding the shovels hoped that colder winter temperatures would freeze the earth solid and stop the landslides.

Years to build and seconds to cross, a Grand Trunk Pacific train crosses Seeley Gulch. *Bulkley Valley Museum, P0330*

A crew of men firmed up the track that ran east out of Telkwa and the trains were then allowed to add passenger cars as far as Rose Lake.

A snowplow was placed in Smithers for use on the tracks between Decker Lake and Smithers. There were two more snowplows west of New Hazelton, one on the lower Skeena and one operating toward Skeena Crossing. Three snowplows were evidently not enough because snow blocked the tracks frequently; several freights were derailed and had to be abandoned temporarily.

Stewart Brothers at Burns Lake finished their contract. Dan Stewart stated that since April 1913 they had moved over eight hundred thousand cubic yards of rock and earth and had on their contract several steam shovels and donkey engines. The four hundred men on that payroll were released from camp and cashed out at New Hazelton. One day at the end of March 1914, FWS paid out $45,000.

The merchants all along the line reported a boom in sales at Christmastime. Sales were made out of retail tents and temporary buildings along the rough Main Street of

Smithers. The many hundreds of men employed near New Hazelton on the tunnels came to that town and purchased record sales of men's clothing.

Stores ordered in Christmas goodies and gifts. The Lynch Brothers, merchants in New Hazelton, Smithers and Prince Rupert, imported boxes of lemons, oranges, apples, currants and nuts for Christmas.

The New Year began with an ominous announcement from Dr. Wrinch that every bed in the Hazelton hospital was full of railroad men. This was due not to a contagious disease but to the many mishaps and accidents along the line. Dr. C.G. McLean in Smithers also reported looking after many of the railroad's sick and injured out of his very rough building in the bustling Smithers townsite.

As work was completed more men packed up their gear and left. Captain McLeod left on a train stuffed with departing labourers to spend the winter at his home in Kincardine, Ontario. Mr Paget, of Shady and Paget, completed his contract of grading ten miles (sixteen kilometres) west of Decker Lake. In nine months he removed 3,000 yards (2,743 metres) of material, including 60,000 yards (54,864 metres) of gumbo. Paget worked straight for those nine months and then took some well-deserved time off after setting a record for the most amount of material moved with just one steam shovel. He headed back to Sunridge, Ontario, expecting to return to work on the PGE in the spring.

Contractors spared no expense to get the job done; one foreman, Mr. Johnston, hired one hundred four-horse teams and moved a steam shovel, engines and track to the last big contract at Fraser Lake.

In early 1914, C.C. Van Arsdol predicted that D.A. Rankin and Company might not be done their large contract at Decker Lake before the tracklayer was at their site. This was the contract where Leslie worked. No contractor wanted to hold back the laying of steel and work at Decker Lake stepped up pace. William Tuck, the "walking boss" for D.A. Rankin and Company and co-worker to Leslie Martin, said Dan Dempsey and his tracklayer suffered only a brief wait while the right-of-way was opened up. Dempsey's track-laying crew moved through D.A. Rankin and Company's contract and went on to Freeburg and Stone's on the east end of Burns Lake.

The Union Bank Robbery of 1913

During the height of railway construction the Union Bank in New Hazelton was handling massive amounts of cash. Considering the large amount of freight being hauled, the merchandise purchased and the many hundreds of men on the Foley, Welch and Stewart payroll, the bank was well supplied with funds.

One mid-November afternoon in 1913, just after dusk, four masked men slipped into the empty Union Bank. When the two employees of the Union Bank, clerk Fenton and cashier McQueen, returned to work after dinner they were greeted with pointed guns. McQueen was shot in the face and fell to the floor while Fenton was forced to open the safe. The robbers removed a large sum of money, ordered Fenton to the floor and ran out the back door disappearing into the surrounding forest. Fenton ran out the front door and alerted the community by firing his gun in the air. Dr. Wrinch at the Hazelton hospital tended to McQueen who was alive but had a bullet lodged in his jaw.

Chief Gannon of the Provincial Police tracked the robbers to the first summit of Roche de Boule Mountain Range where he found several money orders. Winter weather descended on the mountain and the police were forced to turn back. The search was called off, the robbers got away and the bank and its depositors lost over $16,000. The injured McQueen went to Vancouver (some fifty-six hours travel time by horse-drawn stage, train and steamer) to have the bullet removed.

PRINCE RUPERT, BC
NOVEMBER 28, 1913

My Dearest Ruth

Here I am at Doc Orme's new library writing table. Just came in to Prince Rupert tonight to find Les and Doc keeping "bachelor's hall" while Mrs. Orme is in Vancouver showing young Terrence to grandmother.

Your letter was here. I don't deserve one from you. Here I brought this paper and envelope to write you a note en route. But my traveling companions were too numerous. 6:30 am to 8:30 am drives, 9 am to 5 pm train trip, then a cozy stuffy tent, another day trip of 7:30 am to 5 pm.

We will be here just two nights and one day and back to Decker Lake. I could not come out with Les but I tagged along after and will go back with him.

It makes a diversion anyway. I will settle down later.

Bernice

DECKER LAKE
DECEMBER 6, 1913

My Dear Ruth,

The old train is days late. Slides down at Mile 44 (from Rupert) and there has been no mail for a week.

Last week I left here and went to Prince Rupert, a two day RR journey, with one night in the coming city of Smithers. Between the days a birthday dinner for Leslie at Mrs. Parker's, much shopping, a moving picture show etc.

The GTPR is selling the town site of Smithers. Hence the overnight stop there. We slept at Mr. Moran's room over Lynche's Store, "Just pull the bed against the door Leslie for we have no latches yet," that was our host's good night. His good morning, "Eight o'clock Leslie, I'll bring you some water to wash with," enter one basin warm water, one towel, one cake of soap. Oh ye family tub.

The train was three hours late on this end and the driving team in a prancing mood. Les had picked up and mended an old torchlight with a bull's-eye end. It was our salvation that night. Nine miles of bumpity roads and a lickety-split pace. Les held the team down the best he could for it was a new road. Les had not been over it before. We were glad when the nine miles were over and we had reached our home.

The real cold is coming now after the thaw and the lake is booming as it freezes. It is a sheet of glass and I am going to borrow skates and turn out with the crowd tonight. Meanwhile I must finish the Christmas gifts at a reckless rate.

Bushels of love,

Bernice

DECKER LAKE, BC
JANUARY 6, 1914

My dear Ruth,

The New Year is a lovely one up here. Frost and light snow every night and bright, sunshiney days.

Yesterday Leslie drove to camp for the first time this winter down the ice. I drove a mile or more with him and climbed up the bank and onto the sleigh road and walked home. Today I am going down to meet him. Yesterday he ran over one of our precious chickens so we are to have a little feast tonight upon his return.

Our Christmas was lovely. The box arrived two days before and we were not going to open it. But we were sending a box to go to camp. Sent them one of our turkeys, cranberries, can of corn on the cob, olives, jelly, powdered sugar and I looked in your box for a duplicate box of candy to send. Did not encounter any I could possibly spare.

The records are lovely. I feel proud to have such good records in our collection. Your canned goods all came through beautifully.

I made three cookies for Christmastime: royal, gingersnaps and almond cookies.

Have I asked you if you want me to buy any fur pelts? Martin is about $13 for a pelt. Mink are a little less, weasel or ermine, just 75 cents. Reddish fox $8–$10 a piece, two or three to a set. Beaver are not contraband this year and skins are $6. Leslie would like a beaver lined coat but feels we cannot afford it.

Well, kiss all the family all around twice for me.

Bernice

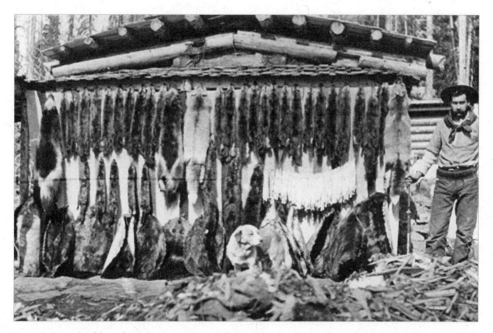

A season's catch of furs along the government telegraph line near Hazelton. *Bulkley Valley Museum, P0536*

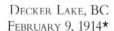

DECKER LAKE, BC
FEBRUARY 9, 1914★

Dear Ruth:

Monday afternoon and the washing, ironing and bread are all finished. Besides all the rest I had the two little Bowness girls all the afternoon. We went walking while the bread was rising. The kiddies (as children in this country are always called) were decked out in my clothes and having the time of their lives.

Tomorrow I am going down to Bosworth's to stay the night and take the train in the morning to Mrs. Dorreen's. Though the train goes some twenty miles beyond here it only takes passengers as far as Rose Lake, nine miles below here. If you have a map and pick out South Bulkley and imagine me there on Wednesday.

I have three-fold purpose in using this machine. First, to write to you. Second, I am too tired to use the pen and tired of the house. Third, I want to practice. Some man was in here the night before when I was copying some recipes. He asked questions and before I knew it Leslie had almost made a dicker to sell the machine. Up here men talk along for a few minutes and presto a few tons of hay have been sold or one man made a promise of something, the promise involving five or six hundred dollars. Dick Carol, who drives a little one-horse affair of a stage, said he "might take it [the typewriter] out to his ranch in the spring for $80."

When we are through here Les thinks we might go to Seward, Alaska. If the Alaska RR bill ever went through. Of course, before we do this, we have promised to stay at the Parkers' in Prince Rupert. No one seems to know when we will be through here though. There is still a small crew of men working at the camp. When they finish Les will have to close and check the camp books, close the general books of D.A. Rankin Company and take them to Hazelton and have them audited and get the money, I hope.

In the meantime he is keeping his eye on his freight outfit of 40 horses which is earning its oats by freighting from the end of steel to the various other contractors who are working east of here.

The entire line is under work from here to Fort George with steel in the town from the other end. The remainder of work lies half and half under this force and the east end force with the worst piece of work in this hundred miles squarely in the middle, the bridge over the Nechako, which Mr. Sprauge is in charge of. Perhaps an engineer might take exception to some of this not being accurate but it is as I hear and conclude.

Goodbye, thanks for the present.

Bernice

EDITOR'S NOTE: All of Bernice's previous letters were handwritten, but this February 9, 1914, letter was written on a typewriter.

Grand Trunk Pacific Railway tracks alongside the port of Prince Rupert. *Northern BC Archives and Special Collections, Prince George Railway and Forestry Museum, Grand Trunk Pacific Railway Collection, 2002.1.21.2*

DECKER LAKE, BC
FEBRUARY 22, 1914

My dear Ruth,

Just at present we dream of building a home in Rupert and a home in Seward, Alaska, and starting a fox farm here at Decker and working on the government road in Alaska. But we have no idea what we will do in reality.

I expect I shall stay in Prince Rupert with Les while the Parkers get a little vacation. Then go to Alaska for a trip and see what's doing. Then I will come home to Fondy.

Les may be hustled right over to the Pacific Great Eastern south of Fort George. In that case, I'd take a trip out while he is getting settled. He feels he cannot go east this year but urges me to take the trip. If I do go I shall farm it with you a good month if you let me.

Bernice

SPRING 1914

"I am no longer surprised at anything. I have seen tea served most formally with a full silver service, in a three-room cabin. I have found Encyclopedia Britannica in a tent."

A special train checks the track for spread rails and sunken ties. *Northern BC Archives and Special Collections, Prince George Railway and Forestry Museum Society, Grand Trunk Pacific Railway Collection, 2002.2.21.35*

Fort Fraser at the east end of Fraser Lake was announced as the site of the joining of the steel and the ceremony of the last spike.

The gravel trains travelled up to Decker Lake, Burns Lake and Fraser Lake and a ballast crew readied the tracks. Heavy freight and passenger traffic was expected over the line as soon as it was completed and the Grand Trunk Pacific (GTP) directed Foley, Welch and Stewart to have the railway up to standards.

Even before the snow had melted, the grading on the GTP had reached the final leg. John Bostrom worked his steam shovels at Decker Lake with dirt flying in all directions. The remaining contractors began shipping their outfits to other parts, some holding the steam shovels, donkey engines, horses and camp supplies in the North while they awaited announcement of contracts for the Pacific Great Eastern railway that would link Vancouver to the GTP at Fort George.

By April 1914 the tracklayer neared Fort Fraser and Dan Dempsey announced he had laid his last rail. On April 6 engineer R.A. Harlow knelt in the spring mud and

The Union Bank Robbery of 1914

As a result of the Union Bank robbery of 1913 residents called for more police and a larger jail. The Union Bank had a new safe installed and the combination was only known by two employees, and even they knew only half the combination.

In the morning hours of April 7, 1914, seven robbers burst into the bank to meet the unlucky clerks Mr. Fenton and Mr. Bishop. Bishop explained he only knew half the combination and could not open the safe. The robbers were delivering blows to Bishop when manager Mr. Tatchell, who was rounding the corner of the bank, heard the noise inside, saw a rifle at the doorway and fired shots in the air to warn the residents. The police were called in but the sharpshooting citizens of Hazelton did not wait for the Provincial Police. Fenton and Bishop threw themselves on the floor inside the bank while bullets were exchanged overhead. When the robbers burst from the bank and ran for the trees the Hazelton men shot three dead and captured three more wounded among the trees. One escaped with the money.

The three captured robbers served twenty years in prison and were deported back to their homeland of Russia. A coroner's jury found the shooting of the three bank robbers was justified. Union Bank manager Mr. Tatchell placed an ad in the *Omenica Herald* stating, "I wish to thank the citizens who risked their life in the fray in connection with the recent bank robbery here, I also wish to warmly congratulate them on their ability to handle such an emergency."

As a result of the second bank robbery in Hazelton in less than six months the police force was expanded, a small addition went on the jail and the Union Bank put bars on their windows and considered moving to a more populated area of town.

Engineer Harlow paints the point of completion on the railway track. *Bulkley Valley Museum, P0336*

marked the point of completion. An equal measurement was taken and the starting lines for the tracklayers from the east and the west were marked.

People travelled from all around; they wanted to see the tracklayers from east and west race to the point of completion and they wanted to witness the last spike ceremony of the Grand Trunk Pacific Railway. A train arrived from the west with prominent railway officials and one train arrived from the east with chairmen, head engineers, board commissioners and managers of the Grand Trunk Pacific Railway.

On April 7, 1914, officials in crisp black suits and hats stood in the mud and the melting snow; behind them stood rows of labourers in overalls. They heard the riot of noise as the tracklayers raced and the crowds of labourers worked on the last section of steel rails on the GTP. A team of men from the east and a team of men from the west raced towards each other. The team from the east won the race.

Short rails were cut and secured in place to bridge the gap and Grand Trunk Pacific president, Edson Chamberlin, drove the last spike in Canada's second transcontinental railway. At a cost of $112,000 per mile, the Grand Trunk Pacific Railway was complete.

The track-laying gang lays ties in place during the race of the tracklayers. *Bulkley Valley Museum, P0346*

After driving the last spike Chamberlin presented a gold watch to each of the two men in charge of the track-laying and R.A. Harlow painted on the last rail, "Point of Competion[sic], April 7, 1914." The rail was later taken up, sliced up into paper-weights, engraved and given to GTP Railway officials.

The main line was cleared of work trains and the president's train headed for Prince Rupert, arriving on April 8, 1914. This was the first train to cross the newly completed line. It had seven coaches and a dining car and was decorated with ribbons. The *Interior News* reported that it swept along the line "like a giant meteor with rainbow trimmings."

Despite strikes, obstacles of terrain and tragedies, the Grand Trunk Pacific Railway was completed in April 1914 and the vision of deceased GTP president Charles Hays was realized.

～

New Hazelton, BC
April 1914

My dear Ruth,
Just a line to tell you we are leaving the country. I'm going to Prince Rupert for a few days. I just hardly believe it.

The two tracklayers met on April 7, 1914, with the team from the east winning the race to the designated point of completion. *Bulkley Valley Museum, P0340*

The first of the regular through trains arriving at Smithers from the east, September 3, 1914. *Bulkley Valley Museum, P1365*

A man I talked to this morning said, "Leslie is on the through train, Mrs. Martin." It gets in here at 10:05 and I get on with my trunks.

I am no longer surprised at anything.

I have seen tea served most formally with a full silver service, in a three-room cabin.

I have found *Encyclopedia Britannica* in a tent.

I have been commanded by a Chinaman, "Go catchee on can stlawberries" so he could make me a cake.

I have entertained the living boss (chief of four drivers in a group of freight wagons) and another time the daughter of the Ministry of Finance for the district of B.C.

I have learned to make bread from a starter of yeast, to use turned butter and say "pack" for carry and understand when the grocer says "six bits" (75 cents).

I have eaten off oilcloth and out of enamelware too often to count.

I have driven 40 to 50 miles a day on roads that could hardly be called such.

People from all around gather to watch the tracklayer from the east and the tracklayer from the west compete to be the first to lay the last rail near Fort Fraser. *Bulkley Valley Museum, P0339*

And there are women of greater education than I have by far, whose experience out mine in the shade. I find that I have not had to rough it at all—according to comparisons with some of the others. They are all educated refined people and seem quite happy living in trunks.

I have had a nice visit here, but am too tired out presently to enjoy anything.

At the hotel here in Hazelton I have had breakfast in bed every day for a week. The very day I had planned to go to Old Town to visit Mrs. Wrinch, the doctor's wife, I was played out. I went to bed and was very sick with la grippe.

The Kerr family here is having a battle royal over the fact that Pa carelessly tipped over the fixative on a batch of files and Ma, tired out in the first place, cried and the mess had to be cleared up.

Mrs. Kerr and I did eventually go to Mrs. Wrinch's for a visit but I did not feel a bit good.

I will be glad to get on the boat and have a rest. I have sent to England for lace handkerchiefs for you.

I am coming home to Fondy this summer. I will be able to get Les down there with me but only for a few days.

Bushels of love,

Bernice MM

ENDINGS

After the completion of the Grand Trunk Pacific the railroaders dispersed and the camps disappeared. In March 1914, the *Omenica Herald* wrote, "The country is undergoing a period of readjustment made necessary by the removal of the construction camps and the excellent market they made for all the farm produce. While in the north the contractors were all good sports and were willing to take a chance on a mining deal, a coal deal or a property deal. Many made considerable money on these sidelines, but now that they are gone the money heretofore so easily obtained will have to come from other directions. A new population must come in."

Most labourers and some contractors expected to move on to the next nearest railway project. In 1914 this was the Pacific Great Eastern, a railway to connect north and south from Vancouver to Prince George. But despite the provincial government's promise in 1913 for the construction to commence, World War I caused a shortage of raw materials, equipment and men. The PGE lacked the financial support it needed and men went elsewhere for work as the Pacific Great Eastern, known as the "Prince George Eventually," stalled in its tracks. The Grand Trunk Pacific started regular freight and passenger service in September 1914. But it too felt the effects of the newly declared war. There was not the movement of freight that had been estimated and the passenger service never reached its anticipated volume.

In 1916 a government inspector estimated the construction of the Grand Trunk Pacific Railway's mountain section had cost a total of $93,307,184—over $112,000

GTP crew. Left to right: railroad lineman Eddie Hole, GTP stenographer Arthur Elliot, blacksmith Bill Underhill, clerk Bob Checkley, cook Yuen, accountant Bud Fisher, roundhouse man Harry Dailing and unidentified man. *Bulkley Valley Museum, P253*

per mile. The Grand Trunk Pacific was severely in debt, cut off from investors in England and not generating money.

Prime Minister Borden not only had the war to deal with, he also had the "railway problem." In 1918 the federal government created a crown corporation known as Canadian National Railways and bought out the bankrupt Grand Trunk Pacific Railway. Also in 1918 the provincial government took over the PGE railway.

Charles Melville Hays's predictions of high traffic never came close to reality. But, thanks to his overestimate of use and stubborn insistence on high construction standards, the railway going through northern BC from Prince George to Prince Rupert is one of the nicest routes to travel. Passengers experience gentle curves, low rises and frequent tunnels along the most stunning scenery: lakes, mountains, the Bulkley River, the Skeena River and the Pacific Ocean.

Railroaders

Some railroaders moved away from the North:

Captain McLeod retired after his work on the Grand Trunk Pacific Railway and went back to his family's farm in Kincardine, Ontario.

Cassius "C.C." Van Arsdol, nicknamed "four-tenths Van" for his stubborn insistence that the grade of the railway not exceed four-tenths of one percent, moved out of the North, settling in Washington. He went on to build a road that connected north and south Idaho with, of course, a 0.4 percent grade making sixty-four turns in 2,000 feet (609 metres). It also was completed at a cost that was twice its original estimate.

Johnny Albi moved to Spokane to be with his family there.

Alma Ross and her mother, the widow Mrs. Ross, moved with Alma's brother Harris to Edmonton, Alberta, where Harris continued to support his sister and mother with a bookkeeping job. Alma Ross was still unmarried in 1916.

Dick "Skookum" Johnson finished his huge 800,000 yards of material fill at Fraser Lake and left northern BC to check out California.

—

Some railroaders were not heard from again:

Mrs. Sprauge, wife of Danley Sprauge, may have moved with her husband on to other railway projects after he completed his bridge building contract over the Nechako River.

The trail of Mrs. Ada Bowness, wife of Frank Bowness, and mother to "the three Bowness girls" (Francis and Marguerite are the two known names) is not found after their roadhouse, called the Traveller's Hotel, moved from Van Arsdol to Decker Lake.

Dan Dempsey, who had been yelling from tracklayers for almost ten years—he ran the track-laying gang through Manitoba and Alberta in 1908—was not heard of again.

—

Some of the labourers and some contractors did stay. They bought land, married and raised families:

Stanley and Bessie Parker, Leslie and Bernice's friends in Prince Rupert, stayed in Prince Rupert where Stanley moved from freighting with horses to shipping with automobiles through his company Pacific Cartage Company. The Parkers had three children and Stanley eventually started an automotive dealership, which became Parker Ford.

John Bostrom received a contract for building the rail yards at Fort Fraser. He and his wife Olga and two young daughters, Filly and Elsie, took up land near Francois Lake. By the fall of 1915 he had broken several hundred acres of new ground and was looking forward to planting in the spring.

Mr. C. Bosworth stayed on and lived at Rose Lake with his wife and son.

Doc Sheehan may have stayed in this area because his son, P.H. Sheehan, married a woman in New Hazelton in 1915 and the groom was escorted through town in a celebratory wheelbarrow parade. The newlyweds bought a ranch in the Kispiox Valley.

R.A. Harlow, who witnessed the driving of the last spike at the point of the GTPR completion, worked on the PGE out of Fort George and eventually settled in Prince Rupert.

———

Other railroaders had financially supported the area's mines and, although they moved away, they returned to check on their investments and visit with friends:

Duncan Ross was one of those contractors who returned often to the North until his sudden death in June 1915. He left behind a wife and four children at the family "ranch" near Victoria.

———

Most railroaders expected to find work on the Pacific Great Eastern:

D.A. Rankin went on to work for Burns and Jordan, contractors on the PGE. His younger brother, Harry Rankin, went south for a little holiday before returning to work on the PGE.

Contractor Mr. Sheady took an extended holiday and his working partner Mr. Paget went out east but both planned to return to the North to work on the PGE.

After working with Foley, Welch and Stewart for nearly twenty years the con-

SS *City of Seattle* departure list, April 1914. *www.ancestry.com*

tracting duo Mr. Freeburg and Mr. Victor Stone went right over to work on the PGE.

Archie McDougall went on to complete the rail yards at Prince Rupert.

Timothy Foley, Patrick Welch and John Stewart, of Foley, Welch and Stewart, attempted to build the Pacific Great Eastern despite World War I, lack of materials and lack of investors. The PGE soon went bankrupt and the incomplete line was turned over to the government and amalgamated into Canadian National Railways along with the Grand Trunk Pacific. Mr. Welch and Mr. Stewart went on to form partnerships with Mr. Bloedel and invested in the forest industry of British Columbia.

The men who did go over to work on the Pacific Great Eastern found the progress slow. Some gave up and looked elsewhere for employment.

In 1952 the first train on the PGE arrived in Prince George, almost forty years after the completion of the GTPR.

Bernice and Leslie Martin

Leslie Frank Martin and Bernice Medbury Martin moved out of northern British Columbia permanently.

On the day of the last spike, April 7, 1914, Leslie and Bernice left Prince Rupert aboard the SS *City of Seattle*. They arrived in Seattle two days later, and then travelled to Fond du Lac, Wisconsin, to visit Leslie's mother and his brother Art. Bernice's sisters and brother were also living there.

Leslie returned to northern British Columbia in May 1914 to finish up his work with D.A. Rankin and Company. He likely helped organize the movement of the railroad equipment to the PGE for D.A. Rankin's contract there. On May 23, 1914, New Hazelton's *Omenica Herald* stated, "Leslie Martin left this morning for Prince Rupert. He expects to be located on the PGE."

If Leslie did return to northern BC to work out of Prince George on the PGE, no trace of his work there was found.

Bernice and Leslie went on to visit southern California where Bernice's father, Chauncey, and mother, Eunice, were living.

Then Leslie and Bernice moved to Seattle, Washington, where Leslie tried to start a new business. The northwestern states had just been unionized and this, coupled with the financial restraints of World War I, resulted in the Martins moving again, this time to California.

In 1919, Chauncey Medbury, Bernice's father, died in California. Also in 1919 Bernice gave birth to a daughter, Lesley Anna Martin. Bernice's newly widowed mother, Eunice, moved with Bernice, Leslie and baby Lesley out of California to their new home in Phoenix, Arizona.

Leslie Martin managed a cotton business in Arizona and in 1922 Bernice gave birth to a son, Frank A. Martin.

Bernice, Leslie, daughter Lesley and son Frank settled in Los Angeles, California. Bernice was very active in the Church of Los Angeles and was proud of her daughter's achievements in the choir. The children benefited from their mother's active membership in their schools in Covina, California.

Leslie Martin died in Los Angeles, California, January 15, 1942, at fifty-nine years of age. Bernice Martin died thirty-one years later, in February 1973 at ninety-one years of age. Bernice and Leslie are buried side by side at the Inglewood Mausoleum in California.

Bernice's daughter Lesley, living in California in 2006, at eighty-seven years of age, recalled her mother's stories of northern British Columbia. She described her father, Leslie Martin, as "a kind man, a hard worker too." As for her mother Lesley had this to say: "She was such a good soul, she loved to talk about her time spent way up there."

Lesley came North in 1979 and donated her mother's letters to the Bulkley Valley Museum in Smithers and the British Columbia Archives in Victoria. She stopped near Decker Lake and searched for her mother and father's cabin but no trace of the home nor the 1913 settlement could be found.

GLOSSARY

BLIND MAN'S HOLIDAY. The time between daylight and candlelight or the hour between the time when one can no longer see to read by the light of the day and before the lighting of the candles.

BLIND PIG. A place for the illegal consumption of alcoholic drinks. Usually a road-house, a poolroom or a hotel that serves alcohol illegally, without a liquor licence.

BOHUNK, BOHUNKE, BOHUNKIE. A disparaging term for a labourer from eastern Europe. From the words *Bo*(hemian) and *Hung*(arian).

BUCKBOARD. An open horse-drawn carriage with four wheels; between the two axles are long, flexible boards whose ends rest directly on the axles. The long springy boards cause passengers to bounce about.

BULKLEY VALLEY. Reference to the valley on either side of the 160-mile (257-kilometre) long Bulkley River. In its widest geographic coverage the term encompasses the area from the Bulkley River headwaters at Bulkley Lake, between Burns Lake and Houston, all the way to Hazelton where the Bulkley River joins the Skeena River. In its narrowest coverage the Bulkley Valley encompasses the area between present-day Houston and Moricetown.

CAISSON. A substructure that is sunk or submerged and permits excavation to proceed inside it. It also provides protection for the workers against water pressure and collapse of soil.

CAYUSE. A small pony.

CHATTELS. Movable personal property.

CHIFFONIER. A narrow, high, chest of drawers or bureau, often with a mirror attached.

CHILBLAINS. An inflammation of the skin followed by itchy irritation on the hands, feet, or ears, resulting from frostbite or exposure to cold.

COMMISSARY. A store that sells food, equipment and supplies to personnel or workers.

CONFINEMENT CASE. A sick person confined to their bed or too unwell to care for themselves.

COWICHAN GUARANTEED EGGS. Early newspapers referred to "Cowichan guaranteed eggs" and "regular eggs." Cowichan eggs were thought to be superior.

DERRICK. A machine for hoisting and moving heavy objects, consisting of a movable boom equipped with cables and pulleys and connected to the base of an upright stationary beam.

DICKER. Make a deal, negotiate the terms of exchange.

DINKEY ENGINE. A small locomotive.

DITCHER. A steam-powered shovel on a flatcar. The ditcher has a long boom used to dig out ditches or remove material. The shovel's bucket swings up and over the boom often dumping the material into open railcars behind it where it will be hauled away to be used as fill somewhere else.

DONKEY ENGINE. A.k.a. dinkey engine.

END OF STEEL. The end of the steel tracks; the furthest point of the completed railway track.

GIN POLE DERRICK. A derrick that has a nearly vertical pole supported by guy ropes; the load is raised on a rope that passes through a pulley at the top and over a winch at the foot.

GO-DEVIL. A horse-drawn logging sled or a railway handcar.

GRADE. The base of the railway tracks, the path or route over which the railway is built.

GRIPS. Freight, carried goods or handbags.

KYOTE A.k.a. coyote. A blasting method used by the GTPR in which both black powder and dynamite was used.

LA GRIPPE, GRIPPE. The flu, a highly contagious viral disease.

MONTENEGRO. Formerly the Republic of Montenegro (meaning "black mountain"): a small, mountainous state in southwest Balkans, bordering Croatia, Bosnia and Herzegovina, Serbia, Albania and the Adriatic Sea.

MUSH. To go or travel, especially through or over deep snow with a dog team and sled.

OVERBREAK. Rock excavated beyond the necessary profile of the tunnel.

PIONEER. The Pioneer was the name of the tracklayer, which consisted of a locomotive and a string of flatcars loaded with ties and rails.

PIP. A spell of sickness, an illness, a general feeling of malaise.

SANDHOG. A labourer who works at tunnelling, or underground in the caissons for constructing bridge piers.

SCOW. A flat-bottomed boat with square sides used for transporting freight.

SHANTY. A hole or large rut on the surface of the ice.

SHOVEL. A steam shovel is a large steam-powered excavating machine designed for lifting and moving material such as rock and soil. It is the earliest type of power shovel.

SIDING. A short piece of track lying parallel to the main railway line that enables trains to pull over to stop and transfer freight or to wait while other trains pass on the main line.

SKINNERS. The drivers of four or six horses or mules, also known as teamsters.

SPEEDER. In Bernice's reference, a small, open-air railway vehicle, with three or four railway track wheels, used for travelling short sections of rail or to and from work sites. Manually powered, operated by pumping.

STEAMBOAT. A.k.a. paddleboat, paddlewheeler, sternwheeler. A flat-bottomed boat driven by a steam engine that uses the paddlewheel to develop thrust for propulsion.

STEAM DONKEY. Common name for the steam-powered engine.

STEAMER. Large ocean-going vessels that travelled between Prince Rupert and Victoria, Vancouver, Seattle, the Queen Charlotte Islands and north to Alaskan ports.

SWAMP FEVER. A viral infection of horses, causing weakness and recurrent fever.

SWING. The term used to describe the four- and six-horse teams used to freight supplies. The teams travelled in a long line of five or six teams with a swing foreman. The freighting was constant, with the supplies going to a designated point where rested horses and a new swing boss were waiting to keep the freight moving.

TAMP. To press down firmly.

TEAMSTERS. The drivers of four or six horses or mules, also known as skinners.

TIMEKEEPER. A person who keeps records of the employees and their hours of work, and also records the time taken to complete the job.

WALKING BOSS. The assistant to the superintendent or subcontractor who supervises several contracts and their labourers. Since these camps are usually separated by some distance, the walking boss is frequently seen walking between them.

Conversion Chart

1 mile = 1.6 kilometres
1 metre = 3.2 feet
1 cubic yard = 27 cubic feet
1 ton (US) = 2,000 pounds

REFERENCES

Numerous sources contributed to the creation of this book. The following books and archival materials were consulted:

Asante, Nadine. *The History of Terrace.* Terrace, BC: Totem Press, 1972.

Ball, Fay, et al. *Pioneer Women.* Smithers, BC: Bulkley Tweedsmuir Women's Institute, 1967.

Barman, Jean. *The West Beyond the West: A History of British Columbia.* Toronto: University of Toronto Press, 1996.

Bennett, Norma V. *Pioneer Legacy: Chronicles of the Lower Skeena River.* 2 vols. Terrace, BC: Dr. R.E.M. Lee Hospital Foundation, 1997–2000.

Bowman, Phyllis. *Whistling Through The West.* Prince Rupert, BC: P. Bowman, 1980.

Downs, Art, ed. *Pioneer Days in British Columbia: A Selection of Historical Articles from BC Outdoors Magazine.* Vols. 1, 3. BC Outdoors, 1973–77.

_____., ed. *Pioneer Days in British Columbia: A Selection of Historical Articles from BC Outdoors Magazine.* Vols. 2, 4. Nanoose Bay, BC: Heritage House Publishing Company Ltd., 1975–79.

Fraser Lake and District Historical Society. *Deeper Roots and Greener Valleys.* Fraser Lake, BC: Fraser Lake District and Historical Society, 1986.

French, C.H. and W. Ware. "BC Post: The Hazelton Post." *The Beaver,* May 1924.

Glen, J., Sr. *Where the Rivers Meet. The Story of the Settlement of the Bulkley Valley.* Duncan, BC: New Rapier Press, 1977.

Grand Trunk Pacific. *Smithers, GTP Freight and Division Headquarters.* 1914. Reprint, Smithers BC: Bulkley Valley Historical and Museum Society, 1979.

Kruisslebrink, Harry. *Smithers: A Railroad Town.* Smithers BC: Bulkley Valley Historical and Museum Society, 2008.

Large, Dr. R. Geddes. *The Skeena, River of Destiny.* Vancouver: Mitchell Press, 1957.

Leonard, Frank. *A Thousand Blunders: The Grand Trunk Pacific Railway Company and Northern British Columbia.* Vancouver: UBC Press, 1996.

Lindstrom, Emma A. *From Riverboats to Railroads.* Terrace, BC: Regional Museum Society, 1992.

Lower, J.W. "The Construction of the Grand Trunk Pacific Railway in British Columbia." *British Columbia Historical Quarterly*, Vol. 4, (1940): 163–181.

MacDonald, James M. "Bleeding Day and Night: The Construction of the Grand Trunk Pacific Railway Across Tsimshian Reserve Lands." *Canadian Journal of Native Studies*, Vol. 10, (1990): 33–69.

MacEwan, Grant. *Pat Burns, Cattle King.* Western Producer Prairie Books, 1979.

McHarg, Sandra, and Maureen Cassidy. *Before Roads and Rails: Pack Trails and Packing in the Upper Skeena Area.* Northwest Community College, 1980.

Mould, Jack. *Stumpfarms and Broadaxe.* Saanichton, BC: Hancock House, 1976.

Olds, Charles Sr. *Looking Back, Down Time and Track.* Prince George, BC: n.p. N.d.

O'Neill, W.J. "Wiggs". *Steamboat Days on the Skeena River.* Kitimat, BC: Northern Sentinel Press, 1960.

Orchard, Imbert. "Martin: The Story of a Young Fur Trader." Sound Heritage Series, no. 30. Victoria, BC: Archives of British Columbia, 1981.

Roseberg, Marjorie, and the Heritage Club. *Bulkley Valley Stories.* N.p. N.d.

Sanford, Barrie. *The Pictorial History of Railroading in British Columbia.* Vancouver, BC: Whitecap Books, 1981.

Terrace Regional Historical Society. *Seventy-five Years of Growth.* Terrace, BC: Terrace Regional Historical Society, 2002.

Turkki, P. *Burns Lake and District.* N.p. 1973.

Weedmark, Lillian. "A Tie Cutter's Diary," *Remember When.* Smithers, BC: *Interior News*, February 23, 1994.

_____. "Barret Ranch," *Remember When*. Smithers, BC: *Interior News*, June 15, 1994.

_____. "Early Business," *Remember When*. Smithers, BC: *Interior News*, October 6, 1993.

_____. "Grand Trunk Pacific Station," *Remember When*. Smithers, BC: *Interior News*, September 8, 1993.

_____. "The Hazelton Bank Robberies," *Remember When*. Smithers, BC: *Interior News*, July 6, 1994.

_____. "Mining," *Remember When*. Smithers, BC: *Interior News*, September 29, 1993.

_____. *Pioneer Women of the Bulkley Valley*. Exhibit Guide. Smithers, BC: Bulkley Valley Historical and Museum Society, 1995.

_____. "Place Names," *Remember When*. Smithers, BC: *Interior News*, March 9, 1994.

_____. "The Provincial Police," *Remember When*. Smithers, BC: *Interior News*, March 30, 1994.

_____. "Winter's Work," *Remember When*. Smithers, BC: *Interior News*, September 10, 1993.

Wicks, Walter. *Memories of the Skeena*. Saanichton, BC: Hancock House, 1976.

MUSEUM SOURCES:

Prince Rupert Regional Archives. Prince Rupert, BC.
Chamber of Commerce Records.
Hood, Florence. Unpublished notes.
Leitch, J.S. *Engineering Digest*. 1969. Prince Rupert Regional Archives, 1985.18. MS 620.
Photograph Binders: The City of Prince Rupert Archival Collection and the Wratthal Collection.

BC Archives. Victoria, BC
Martin, Bernice Medbury. *The Letters of Bernice Medbury Martin 1912–14*. BC Archives. MS 1192.

Bulkley Valley Museum, Smithers, BC
BV Museum. Bulkley Valley Place Names Chart. Reference material.
BV Museum. Negative Collection: Negatives F30–F47, F251–F255.
BV Museum. Photograph Collection Index. Photographs 1988–2000.
Grand Trunk Pacific Railway. "Map of the Central Interior of British Columbia Shewing [sic] the Country Served by the Grand Trunk Pacific Railway." Copy. Unaccessioned.

Grand Trunk Pacific Railway. Timetable. Unaccessioned reference.

Jennings, Duncan. Jennings Fonds.

Martin, Bernice Medbury. The Vaniman Donation. 1983.67. 1–120. File 1 of 1. File 2 of 2.

McInness Family Fonds.

Morice, Father. Father Morice OMI, Map of the Northern Interior. Victoria, BC, 1907. Copy. Unaccessioned.

O'Neill, Wiggs. O'Neill Fonds.

Sedgewick, J.K., Chronology of New Caledonia. Copy. Unaccessioned.

Smithers District Board of Trade. Mining Pamphlet for the Bulkley Valley. Smithers, BC: *Interior News*. Part of the Smithers Miners and Prospectors Fonds.

Talbot, F.A. The Labour and Time-Saving Tracklayer and Its Work. 1914.

Talbot, F.A. "The New Garden of Canada." Copy. Unaccessioned.

The Exploration Place, Prince George, BC
Photograph Collection.

Hazelton Pioneer Museum, Hazelton, BC.
Reference Collection. Unaccessioned.

Telkwa Museum, Telkwa, BC.
Photograph Collection.
Reference Library. Unaccessioned.

University of Northern British Columbia, Prince George, BC.
Prince George Railway and Forestry Museum photo collection.
Harlow Collection. Box 29. Box 32. 2002. 1. 30.

ARCHIVAL NEWSPAPERS:
Interior News, Bulkley Valley Museum.
Omenica Herald, Bulkley Valley Museum and the Terrace Public Library.
Omenica Miner, Bulkley Valley Museum and Terrace Public Library.
Prince Rupert Empire, Prince Rupert Library.
Terrace Standard, Terrace Public Library.

Index

Albi, Johnny, 46, 97, 117, 135, 185

Aldermere, 49, 58, 67–**68**–69, 75, **99**, 104, 122

Barrett, Charles, 65, 68, 123, 127

Barrett Ranch, The, 121–24, **133**, **137**

Bloedel, Julius, 188

Boo Family, The, 83, **85–86**, 90, **102**, **108**

Bostrom, John, 25, 46, 97, 110, 135, 173, 186

Bosworth, C., 169, 186

Bowness, Mrs., **26**, **102**–103, **111**, 185

Bulkley Valley, 49, 64–65, 68, 77, 97–99, 104, 120, 150, 152

Burns, Patrick, **72**–73, 79, 103, 132, 138

Burns Lake, 46, 61–62, 66–70, **77**, 86, 97–98, 117–19, 135–36, 145, 156, **163**–65, 173

Chamberlin, Edson, 175, 178

Chicken Lake, 75, 97, 120, 131, 133

Chinese workers, **29**, 31, 43, 121, 146

Conveyor, The, 89, 117

Decker Lake, 58, **67**–68, **77**–78, 81, 86–87, **93**, 97–**102**–103, 110–**111**, 117–**121**, **123**, 131–33, 135–36, 143–44, 153, **156**, 161–62, 164–65

Dempsey, Dan, 20, **32**, 39, 51–**52**, **53**, 55, 131, 142, **148**, 150–51, 163, 165, 173, 185

Diamond D Ranch, **65**, 132–**33**–34, **137**

Doughty, Lady and Sir, **143**

DuVernet, Bishop Frederick Herbert, 132

Edgar, Magnus, 162

Ehlrich, Mrs., 78, **80**

Ehlrich, Mr., 49

Foley, Welch & Stewart, 21–22, 30–31, 36, 56, 61, 63, 66, 70, 74–75, 90, **99**–100, 117, 135, 151, **156**, 158, 186, 188

Finnish workers, 29

First Nations, 20, 45, 49, 85, 90

Fort Fraser, 18, 81, 135, 173 **180–81**, 186

French Canadian workers, 29

GTP Steamship Service, 109

Hardscrabble, 24–25, 31, 34, 37, **45**–46, 57, 101, 150–51

Harlow, R.A., 122, 173, **175**, 178, 186

Hays, Charles Melville, 15, 20, 56, 58, 178, 184

Hazelton, 21, 23, **29**, 34, 45–47, **53**, 56, **61**–62, 64, 66–68, **74**–75, 77–78, 81, 91, 96–97, 99–101, 103, 106, 113, 116–22, 130–35, 142–43, 151, 153, 155, 161–62, 164–66, **169**, 174, 188

Hinton, W.P., 118

Hubert, 81, 104, 131

Industrial Workers of the World (IWW) 47–48, 66

Japanese workers, 29

Jasper, Bill, 132–33

Johnson, Dick "Skookum," 98, 107–108, 136, 185

Kelly, John, 145

Kelliher, B.B., 62, 89, 118, 147

Kitselas Canyon, 18, 21, **23**–25, **33**, **39**

Labour conditions, **7**, 17, 20–21, **29**–30, 36, **40–41**, 47–49, 61, 66, 75, 98–99, **114–15**, 131, 135, 153, 162–63, **176–77**, 185

Laurier, Wilfred (Prime Minister), 15

Leitch, John Strickland, 27–28, 33

Little, George, **139**

Martin, Bernice Medbury, **7**, **12**, **92–93**, **123**

Martin, Leslie, **14**, **111**

McInnes, Archie and Neil, 106–107, 133

McLeod, Captain, 25, 63, 82, 98, 123, **150**, 165, 185

Mining, 17, 64, 66, 81, 120, 153

Moncton, New Brunswick, 15–16

Mud Creek, 96, 162

New Hazelton Mine Owners Association, 153

O'Neill, W.J. "Wiggs," 29–30, 36, 113, 132

Pacific Great Eastern Railroad, 143, 152, 171, 173, 183, 186, 188

Paget, Mr., 96, 123, 165, 186

Parker, Stanley and Bessie, **26**, 28, 125, 159, 186

Pioneer Tracklayer, **53**

Port Simpson GTP, The, **56**–57

Popcorn Kate, 125–27

Prince Rupert, **10**, 14–**15**–18, 20–21, **26**, 31, 49, 56, 61, 64, 66, 74–75, 79–81, 84, 109, 113, 118–122, 124, 131, 135, 143, **171**, 178–**79**, 184

Rankin, D.A., 48, 50, 52, 54–**55**, 57–58, 70, 78, 84, 91, 94, 100, 117, 135, 139, 153, 158, 165, 170, 186

Rankin, Harry, 37, 70, 156, 186

Roadhouses, 49, 83–84, 107, 120, **126**–27, 138

Ross, Mrs., **12**, 32, 59, 107, **123**, 185

Ross, Duncan, 46, 82, 132, 151, 186

Scottish workers, 29

Seeley Gulch, 66, 78, **164**

Sheady, Mr., 153, 186

Sheehan, Doc, 90, 119–20, 186

Skeena Crossing Bridge, 25, **52**, **62**–**63**, 78

Skeena River, 13, 16, 18, 20–**22**–25, 28–30, 32, 36, 38–**39**, 45–**47**, **52**, **56**, 63–64, 77–78, 117–18, 130, 150

Smithers, 69, **81**, **96**–97, 104–**105**, 120, 131–32, **134**, **147**, 150, **152**, **154**, **157**, 162, 164–65, 167, **182**, 189

Smithers, Sir Alfred Waldon, 104, **143**

Sprauge, Mrs., **12**, 79–**80**, 88, **123**, 185

Sprauge, Danley D., 79, 88, 146–47, 170, 185

SS *City of Seattle*, The, 188

SS *Prince Rupert*, The, 109, **113**

Stewart, John W., 21–22, 100, 118, 135–36, 151, 188

Telkwa, 21, 46, 49, 64, 67, **69**, **70**, 77, 81, 97, 104, 113, 116, 120, 131, **140**, **148**, **150**, 152, 161, 164

Telkwa River, 120, **131**, **135**, 142

Terrace, **36**, 56, 139

Tuck, William, 58, 70, 139, 156, 165

Tunnelling, 29, **33**

Union Bank, The, 166, 174

Van Arsdol, Cassius "C.C.," 25, 89, 165, 185

Wicks, Walter, 29–30, 36, 106

Winnipeg, Manitoba, 15–16

ACKNOWLEDGEMENTS

This book would not have been possible without the knowledgeable staff and dedicated volunteers at the museums, libraries and archives throughout the Northwest. Thanks are due to Prince Rupert Archives, Prince Rupert Library, Terrace Library, Hazelton Pioneer Museum, Hazelton Library, Bulkley Valley Museum, Bulkley Valley Genealogical Society, Telkwa Museum Society, University of Northern British Columbia Archives, Prince George Railway and Forestry Museum, Prince George's Exploration Place and the Valley Museum and Archives in McBride. Thanks also to the staff at BC Archives in Victoria for their prompt replies.

I am grateful to Frank Leonard for digging through his personal archives to satisfy my curiosity and for reading this manuscript. Thanks to many local historians too numerous to list here who kindly returned my phone calls and shared their knowledge.

For help along the way: Tom Grasmeyer, Mary Andersen, Christy Hall, Stewart Young and Patsy Young.

Thanks also to the Bulkley Valley Community Arts Council in Smithers.

I am grateful to Lorna Townsend for steering me to Caitlin Press. Thanks are due to the Caitlin Press team: Vici Johnstone for her expertise, Erin Schopfer for carefully editing the manuscript, Michelle Winegar for designing an attractive book and thanks also to my neighbour Hans Saefkow for a really great map.

Thanks to my friends and extended family for their enthusiasm. A special thanks to my husband John for his support and my children for their constant motivation—"Now are you done writing your book, Mama? Now are you done? Mama, are you done yet?"